D0966456

The Power
of Partnerships

I would like to dedicate this book to my wonderful mother, Lillian Mariotti Kiss, who passed away before she could read it but whose beliefs, principles, and spirit are wrapped in every page.

The Power of Partnerships

THE NEXT STEP

Beyond TQM,

Reengineering

and Lean Production

John L. Mariotti

Copyright ©   John L. Mariotti, 1996

The right of John L. Mariotti to be identified as author of this work has been asserted in accordance with the Copyright, Designs and Patents Act 1988.

First published 1996

Blackwell Publishers, a publishing imprint of
Basil Blackwell Inc.
238 Main Street
Cambridge, Massachusetts 02142
USA

Basil Blackwell Ltd.
108 Cowley Road
Oxford OX4 1JF
UK

Library of Congress Cataloging-in-Publication Data
Mariotti, John L., 1941-
    The power of partnerships : the next step beyond TQM, reengineering and lean production : a competitive cornerstone for the 21st century / John L. Mariotti.
        p.   cm.
    ISBN 1-55786-717-8
    1. Industrial management.   2. Performance contracts.   I. Title.
    HD38.M326   1996
    658–dc20   95-1579
                                                                                     CIP
British Library Cataloguing in Publication Data
A CIP catalogue record for this book is available from the British Library

Typeset by Megan H. Zuckerman

Printed in the USA by Book Crafters

This book is printed on acid-free paper

About the Author

John L. Mariotti's career spans 30 years of diverse business experience in four different industries. During the past year, Mariotti founded *The Enterprise Group*, a coalition of *Time-shared Executive Advisors©* and *The Center for Partnership Development™,* an organization to assist companies in forming successful partnerships. He also holds an appointment at the University of Tennessee College of Business as Director, Corporate Relations. He has been listed in Who's Who in International Business, and has spoken of his business experiences to thousands of people over the past ten years.

Most recently he was President of Rubbermaid's Office Products Group of three U. S. and six international operations spanning North America, Europe, Asia, and Australia. Prior to this, Mariotti was President of Huffy Bicycles, the leading U. S. brand and world's largest producer of bicycles. He joined Huffy in 1979 as President and General Manager of their Oklahoma Bicycle Division.

Mariotti began his career with Automatic Electric Company, the manufacturing arm of GTE. He spent twelve years at L.R. Nelson Corporation, a privately held watering products manufacturer where he held all major operations responsibilities, before becoming V. P. Planning & Development. Mariotti holds B.S. & M.S. degrees in Mechanical Engineering from Bradley University and the University of Wisconsin.

Contents

Preface

Someone asked me the other day, "What makes a person undertake such an ambitious project as writing a book?" I was not sure what drives many authors to persist until they have translated their thoughts into the written word, but I began thinking about why I wanted to write this particular book, on this rather obvious topic.

Over the past 30 years, I have seen a lot of management and leadership styles. Some I admired and others I thought were simply awful. Many were just mediocre. I have believed for many years that partnering with someone, some company, or some group was the best way to achieve a goal that could benefit both. More specifically, I believe there is a way to do it that is right and a way that is wrong. Fortunately, Stephen R. Covey saved me the task of coining names for the right way and the wrong way in his best-selling book, *The Seven Habits of Highly Effective People* [1]. He called one way (type of leadership) *principle based* and another type *personality based*. The right way to do things, in partnerships, management, leadership, or life, is based on principles! The wrong way is based on personality. To put this in simple terms: a principle-based person (leader, manager, partner) *does things that are right because they are right.* Principles are deep, fundamental truths – not negotiable. Personality-based people do things because they will look good, seem right (sometimes they happen to be right), and create a favorable image.

Unfortunately, personality-based people feel everything is negotiable, and they lack the deep-rooted beliefs and values principles provide. They sort of go with the flow – to look good. People who work or live around them, sooner or later, discover this. An oft-used, old fashioned term was *fair-weather friends,* and it fit these people some of the time. The problem, you see, with people not guided by principles, people who are steered by personality, is that they cannot be trusted – period. Their organizations figure that out pretty quick. So do their "friends," and as a result, they run in flocks. "There's safety in numbers," the old cliché says. I wanted to write this book because this all needed to be said and in one place. Many admirable people contributed unknowingly to the content of my effort. I hope I have accurately quoted them and recognized the quality of their thoughts. I cannot say with certainty that everyone I quoted was a principle-based person, only that they *talked the talk.* Most of them, I suspect, also *walk the talk.* The concept of business partnerships in the fullest, most integrative sense deserved a broad, in-depth description. So did the way to do it, based on principles, trust, trustworthiness, character, competence, persistence, integrity, honor, and humanity.

I would like to add a note at the outset. Often, people confuse the right way of doing things as "just being nice," but there is more to it than that. *Nice* is an acceptable way to think of it as long as the word *tough* is not forgotten. *Toughness* in my context means having a competitive spirit, determination, and the willingness to face and deal with difficult situations and people. Since it is easy to be "tough" in a mean-spirited way, I will not dwell on it too often in the rest of the book – but do not forget it. Many of the people whose styles led to successful partnerships were nice *and* tough both, as the situation called for each – like Sam Walton or Vince Lombardi. This short Preface has already become too long, so now that I have described the "why," let us get on with the rest.

I find myself putting down many of the recent "good advice" business books after reading the first few chapters or halfway through. One characteristic of the 1990s is conflicting demands on our time. Although reading a book is an excellent way to pass the time in an airport or on a vacation, it often gets shoved aside in the day-to-day pressure of phone calls, correspondence, and personal encounters. Because of that, this book will be short and organized somewhat like a newspaper. Some important thoughts will be outlined at the start of each chapter with the major part of its text filling out the "ations" (explanation, justification, clarification, and pontification!). I find that really useful books I read end up with a lot of dog-eared pages and notes in the margin. I hope there is enough "white space" around the words here for the readers who are so inclined to write notes in the margins and make this a real tool for improvement and success. Because thick books take up a lot of room in the briefcase or suitcase and are heavy to carry around, I always prefer thinner books with a higher quality-to-quantity ratio. I will try to make this book one of that kind.

Numerous people have inspired me and assisted me in the preparation of this book. I would like to thank them all but especially Tom Peters for his conceptual motivation; Bill Lake, Tony Morreale, and Tom Kappa who reviewed chapters in progress; and Doug Dempsey, Jim

Barber, Ed Holzer, Mike Stahl, Rick Maurer, Jack Kahl, Michael Kami, Ram Charan, and my son Michael for reviewing "the whole thing" and providing their valued input. I would also like the thank a man I have never met but whose wisdom on the subjects of business, management, and leadership over the past three or four decades has shaped much of my thinking, Peter Drucker. Most of all, I would like to recognize and thank my wife Maureen and all three of our children, Lisa, Mike, and Susan, who supported and inspired me while tolerating numerous interruptions to our life so I could record these thoughts.

Introduction

- We can learn from the successes and failures of others.
- "What" is easy, "how" is hard.
- Change is the only constant in these times.
- Partnership allows us to change as rapidly as we must.
- Business partnerships are like marriages – many fail.

One characteristic of the 1980s and 1990s is an explosion of books prescribing a "magic pill" or quick fix solution for businesses. Tom Peters and Bob Waterman popularized the business case study with their widely read book *In Search of Excellence* [2]. While they have taken a lot of criticism for the failures of their "excellent" companies, I think they are to be commended for calling attention to the entire topic of business success for other than just serious business readers. (I also believe that the whole topic of excellence is a matter of timing – today's excellent company may not be that tomorrow, unless it adapts and reconfigures itself to be excellent in rapidly changing conditions.)

This book is written primarily for the business reader, but will be worthwhile for the casual reader who is interested in the basis for success in a wide variety of situations. As I said earlier, it will be short, not long. It will not be packed with amazing case studies, simply because each situation is different. A couple of simple examples with some explanation are all that is required to illustrate these principles. I have tried to fold in some of my own experiences over the past 30 years in the hope that the reader can learn from them as I have. After that, it is the job of the business managers or executives to adapt the principles of partnership to their own specific situation.

As in life, "what" to do is often fairly obvious or simple. "How" to do it, and the hard work, discipline, know-how, and persistence to get it done are the challenges. The how and the doing it are hard, but difficulty should be an attraction not a deterrent. As Tom Hanks's character, the manager, in the movie *A League of Their Own*, told one of his players: "Hard is good. That's how we win. If it was easy, everybody would be doing it!"

Partnerships as I will discuss them in this book are defined as relationships between companies and people who share common goals, strive to achieve them together, and do so in a spirit of cooperation, collaboration, and fairness. *There does not need be shared ownership to have a partnership.* Many alliances are "nonequity" in the ownership sense. Many situations are based on "mutual dependence," and one of the most obvious questions is whether those are really partnerships. The answer is "maybe," depending on how the parties behave and view their relationship. Many, in fact, far too many, are "marriages of convenience" (or necessity) and that is all they are! Certainly, a lot is at stake regardless of the reasons behind these relationships or their legal boundaries. I will use a simple description to make it easy for people to relate to the topic business partnerships. A business partnership is a collaborative alliance of people from interdependent groups – teams, peers, customers, suppliers [3]. This rightfully describes many of the partnerships I will examine, but it can be too limiting in an overall sense, because partnerships can go far beyond the world of business!

My father was a professional musician who had his own band or orchestra from the time he was 16 years old. I know the interaction among the musicians in his band was a partnership. He once told me that the real test of how "together" they were was not that they started together, nor that they played together during the tune – although that was critical for the music to sound good – but rather that they all finished together. That was the true test of their unity or partnership. Perhaps that little story has a deeper message than I thought at the time.

Business partnerships should be approached in the same way as marriages. They go through stages: euphoria, routine, adjustments, (sometimes) difficulties, and then acceptance, followed by fulfillment. Both are relationships that, if done well, create a total that is greater than the sum of the parts. Both are often tried. Some fail. Some succeed. Over time, the partners grow together or they grow further apart. The process, the give and take, the hopes for success, and the determination to make it work are all necessary parts of getting there.

I hope you will find many useful insights on "how" and the encouragement to persist, to keep doing it, until you are successful (or until you conclude that it cannot work!). Of all the relationships and principles I have encountered in over 30 years of management and leadership positions, none has come close the power of partnerships. The power of alliances and partnerships and the concept of reconfiguration of the business to meet constantly changing competitive conditions (which goes beyond the scope of this book) hold the secret to lasting success in most businesses and organizations. Without any further delay, let us get into the why of partnerships and (nonequity) alliances and see how they fit into the plethora of buzz-word solutions that managers and executives grasp at futilely to deal with the problems of the modern business enterprise and achieve competitive success.

Prologue

The year was 1984. The U.S. bicycle market was under attack by the Taiwanese. Prices both at the retail and wholesale levels were dropping more than 1 percent every month. Imported bikes, which had reached a low point in 1982 at 16 percent of the U.S. market, would blow past the 25 percent level, headed for a high of 57 percent in 1987. New Taiwanese "makers" were springing up like weeds after a spring rain. The number would reach over 100 before the battle reached its peak. This was nothing new for the U.S. bike manufacturers. About every 10 to 15 years another country would come after this large, lucrative ($1 billion plus), and relatively open market. It was Europe in the 1950s and 1960s, then Japan in the 1970s, and now Taiwan, with Korea warming up to be next, and the monster of China lurking in the shadows just over the horizon.

In 1982–83, the recession in the United States, combined with the advent of the new video games, siphoned away purchasing dollars and caused the U.S. bike market to hit bottom at just under 7 million units annually. This was down from the 1979 peak of almost 11 million. In the late 1970s, U.S. manufacturers had been clamoring to add capacity just to supply the continuously rising demand. The market had doubled in size every decade for the past 40 years and peaked with the discovery of the ten-speed racer in the early 1970s. This uncomfortable, relatively fragile machine imported from Europe caught the fancy of U.S. gas-starved, recreation- and fitness-focused population and drove the U.S. market past the 14 million bike point in 1973, only to crash to just half that level by 1975.

The U.S. bike manufacturers not wiped out by that collapse were likely to fall to the one in the early 1980s. Any that survived were left to face the attack of the Taiwanese with a labor force paid less than $1.00/hour and a burgeoning bicycle component industry rapidly migrating there from Japan (where autos and electronics were becoming king). It was this intimidating scenario that we faced at Huffy Bicycles in 1984.

Ten-speed bikes were selling fine at retail prices of $89–99, with an occasional promotion at $79 in the early 1980s. Kids' 16" and 20" (wheel) bikes were often priced at $59–69 and seldom promoted below $50. Features were minimal, amenities few. Then came the Taiwan imports, sporting the features that had been yielding $10–20 or more in retail premiums. Worst of all, these bikes landed in the United States with styling and paint jobs that looked good, at prices that let discount retailers like Target and Zayre sell ten speeds at $69 with better margins than their domestic counterparts at $79! Just as the U.S. manufacturers figured out how to squeeze down their costs and (especially) their margins to compete at this level, retail prices dropped again – to $59 for ten speeds and $49 for kids' bikes! The U.S. dollar had strengthened until it was worth 40 of the NT$ (New Taiwan dollar), and aggressive U.S. discount buyers and importers were having a field day.

In 1983, Huffy held 22 percent of the U.S. bike market. Imports were still below 20 percent. By 1987, Huffy still held 22 percent, imports were at 57 percent. In 1991, imports were sliding below the 45 percent mark, the U.S. dollar was worth only 25 NT$, and Huffy was up to 33 percent share (limited only by its capacity to produce). The bottom of the price slide had seen wholesale prices drop over 25 percent. Huffy had maintained its share and profitability by reducing costs almost the same amount. The question was, How?

The answer is not so simple as a single word, but one word sums up the pivotal common denominator of it: Partnerships! Huffy Bicycles had formed a cooperative "partnership" with its 2,000 employees and with the leaders of the United Steel Workers, their union. It formed partnerships with (a reduced number of) the best suppliers both in the United States and abroad. It formed partnerships with a select group of leading retailers like Wal*Mart, Toys R Us, Kmart, Target, Price Club, Cotter & Co. (True-Value Hardware), regional discounters like Pamida, Meijer, Caldor, and many others. Huffy had also formed partnerships with a small, select group of outside resources to help shape its strategic thrust, including Ram Charan, Roger Blackwell, Andersen Consulting, Mitchell Fein (the founder of Improshare), Lois USA advertising, and the local and state governments and educational institutions in Ohio.

These partnerships alone would not have been sufficient if it were not for a lot of hard work, innovation, cooperation, and more than a little luck. But one thing is certain: without these partners, their support, and the combined power of them pulling together, the history of Huffy Bicycles, and in fact, Huffy Corporation, would be very different indeed.

Chapter 1

The Critical Partnerships

KEY POINTS

- Four partnerships are critical.
- High-quality materials make high-quality products.
- Nothing happens until a sale is made.
- Think win-win in relationships to build partnerships.
- The importance and power of partnerships are being recognized.

Four partnerships are the most cirtical to any success-ful venture – the partnership with a supplier, with a cus-tomer, with employees or associates, and with that valued, special partner, be it personal or professional.

These partnerships are founded on six common attri-butes. The first four are basic principles of human interac-tion and last two are fundamental business perspectives:

1. *Character* – the combination of qualities or features that distinguishes one person, group, or thing from another.

   Integrity – steadfast adherence to a strict moral or ethical code.

   Honesty – marked by or displaying integrity, upright; not deceptive or fraudulent, genuine; characterized by truth, not false: sincere, frank.

2. *Trust* – firm reliance on the integrity, ability, or character of a person or thing.

3. *Open communication* – a process by which information and ideas are exchanged freely between two parties..

4. *Fairness* – having or exhibiting a disposition that is free of favoritism or bias, impartial; just to all parties, equitable.

5. *Self-interest of both partners* – there must be "something in it" of an economic or otherwise beneficial nature for both partners.

6. *Balance of rewards vs. risks and / or resources required* – the partnership cannot be too lopsided.

Supplier Partnerships

A law of physics says that matter can neither be cre-ated nor destroyed. In the context of these thoughts, it could also be expressed as "you cannot make something from nothing!" This principle expresses the importance of a supplier partner in its most basic form. Suppliers are usually people who provide materials or parts, but they also might provide services or information. Whichever is the case, try to conduct your business without someone to provide you the raw material and/or information to which you will add your particular value and then sell to a customer. It is pretty difficult! In fact, one of the common characteristics of many high-quality companies in business today is that they also use the highest quality materials and develop the best suppliers. Is it a coincidence? I doubt it!

I could name a dozen or more, but I will single out just one for illustration. While I was at Huffy Bicycles, we were fortunate to have a great corrugated carton supplier, Inland Container. This supplier proved just how powerful a partnership can be. Inland had a plant in Middletown, Ohio, just about 100 miles south of our plant in Celina. When we decided to shrink our supplier base and really concentrate on partnerships with the biggest or the best supplier, Inland was our choice for our *sole supplier* of cartons. When you make over 15,000 bikes a day, running out of cartons can stop the whole plant. We sent a team of engineers and quality professionals to "survey" the plant and the few things found to be less than excellent at the plant were quickly improved.

As time went by, the company not only measured up to the task, but exceeded most of our expectations. The plant continued to improve such that our regular follow-up surveys were mostly perfunctory. We did, however, continue to hold "mutual appreciation" meetings every year, where management from the executive to the working level gathered to reflect on and celebrate the success and build the strength of the partnership. Not only did Inland meet our production needs, but it actively participated in value analysis to help us continue removing unnecessary costs from our packaging materials. In this case, two "Bills," our Vice President Bill Lake and Inland's now retired Vice President Bill Long, were the architects of the partnership. Remember this when we get back to where partnerships start – with people.

Employee or Associate Partnerships

If you are the owner of a business, an executive, manager, professional, or "just an employee(!)," you have probably already discovered the importance of partnerships. One of the most rewarding partnerships is with other employees, or "associates" as many of the forward thinking companies call them. As you might imagine, I really like the term used by Manco, Inc. They call them *partners*! (They really are, since Manco is an employee owned company.) We never quite got to the point of changing the name from employees to something else at Huffy, but they were always known as "Huffy's people"! At Rubbermaid, we called employees our associates. I am not sure if that was one of Stanley Gault's legacies or if it preceded him from Don Noble, who shaped a lot of Rubbermaid's excellence before Gault got there. It is a lot easier to point out the importance of everyone's role in a business if they can all be thought of as "associates" or "partners."

I'll never forget an incident in the factory at Huffy several years ago that helped clarify the differing roles of associates. I was talking to one of the experienced men who worked in our "painted frame and fork" focused factory. I was commenting how much I would like to spend more time out in the factory, even working at some of the jobs more than I had (over the years I had tried many of them, but just briefly). He told me, in no uncertain terms, that "everyone appreciates your willingness to get your hands dirty, but that isn't your role. We will take care of that part of the business [building the product] if you will be sure to take care of yours – which is devising a strategy and plans that would win and making sure everyone is pulling together to execute it." I do not know if he will ever read this, but if he does, "Thanks, Jay!"

Fairness, from manufacturing to management, is one of the most essential attributes, and perhaps the one I would choose, if forced, to describe *the* ideal attribute of partnerships. I once raised a question in an employee forum: What is the definition of a *fair deal*? Probably the best answer I received was, "A deal you'd take either side of." The person who answered, elaborated: "Don't sell a horse you wouldn't buy!" Pretty clear isn't it?

When I took over at the Celina, Ohio, operation of Huffy Bicycles, one of the first meetings I called was with the United Steel Workers union (USW) committee members who represented the people in our plant. The union representatives were not sure what message to expect. I was very clear about what I wanted to tell them, and it was very simple. The Celino, Ohio, plant was the sole survivor of three bicycle divisions of Huffy, one of which I had put a lot of effort into building only to close it. I never wanted to do that again! I told them, "I'll never lie to you, although I won't always tell you everything, because some things are better not known. I will tell you as much as I can about how things are going and how we're doing – whether it's good or bad. It's been like a 'running gunfight' around here for the past few years, but I hope those days are over. I'm 'laying my guns on the table.' If you 'shoot me,' we'll both die. If you work with me, we can both win. The choice is up to you." Thanks to some hard work by my associates, some real forward thinking and learning by the local union officers, and great support from a couple of the United Steel Workers district and national officers, we were able to work together very successfully. Lynn Williams, who was the president of the USW, and Frank Vickers, who was the district director for several years, including my last few at Huffy, were as supportive as any union officers anywhere could have been. Fairness works – and it is a two-way street!

Customer Partnerships

A sign on an office wall I once visited said, "Nothing happens until a sale is made." Marketing authority and Harvard professor Theodore Levitt says it very well in his book, *The Marketing Imagination* [4], "The purpose of a business is to create and keep a customer."

I can think of no simpler, more direct way to say it. Without someone to "buy" what it is we have to "sell," there would be little point in the existence of our business enterprise. Another sign that always intrigued me was the two most important rules regarding customers. Rule number one, the customer is always right. Rule number two, when the customer is wrong, refer to rule number one. Another way to say this is sometimes it is hard to live with them, but it is virtually impossible to live without them. The best way to live with them is as partners, not just as customers.

I could cite a lot of great partnership stories here. One of the best partnerships was the development of the international bike business with Toys R Us and Huffy Bicycles. The collaboration yielded great benefits for both. Toys R Us had the innovative, TV-advertised new (U.S.) bikes in their stores worldwide; bikes made to meet the standards in all the countries where it had stores. In turn, Huffy gained international sales and brand exposure throughout the world. We learned what sold and what did not, and were able to expand our sales and brand presence all over the world. The same sort of partnership worked equally well for Toys R Us stores located in the United States.

Another example was the growth of Huffy's business with Wal*Mart. A principle I liked to use was "satisfy the most demanding customer-partner, and you can satisfy nearly everybody else." Wal*Mart's distribution system was by far the most advanced in discount retailing, and their size and growth made some of the demands pretty staggering. If we could partner with Wal*Mart to meet and satisfy their needs, we could probably handle anything or meet anybody else's needs. Since we became Wal*Mart's largest bike supplier for the last six of my Huffy years, (the race was usually with Toys R Us to see who would be our largest customer) it must have worked.

In the Office Products Group of Rubbermaid, we were building a similar partnership with United Stationers, the largest distributor of office products in the United States. The advantages of such a partnership are many – open exchange of information, joint promotional and show ideas, special product promotions, and much more comes out of such partnerships. One of the greatest benefits of this partnership was a better understanding of the respective needs of the two partners was. Such partnerships are not always easy to start nor are they trouble-free. Partnerships are the best way I have found of building a relationship that makes the pressure of a high-paced business environment positive and enjoyable.

Special Partnerships

Special partnerships are of two types, professional partnerships and personal partnerships. Either or both of these may have been a critical factor in most success stories. So many different kinds of partnerships fall under this category that the imagination is the only limit. Even competitors partner with each other to win out over more fearsome competitors or to protect their industry from an external threat. Long-term advisors, local, state or federal governments, universities, consultants – the list is almost endless. Usually, it is the special personal partners who wield the most influence. That special personal partner could be a spouse, a trusted friend, or a business partner (in the professional sense). It could also have been a valued consultant, a mentor, a "boss," or it might be someone in your community, club, or church. I know that every successful person I have met has one or more of these special partnerships, which they all value highly and see as instrumental to their success.

Partnerships are the Best Route to Success

Why do partnerships beat the other ways of achieving success? In a few words, they are more effective, more enjoyable, and easier! For the most part, human beings are fundamentally averse to conflict or at least most are. They do not like anxiety or uncertainty. In my experience, there are fewer loners than joiners or participants. Perhaps there is something in our evolution from the tribalistic rituals of the primitive human development. Wherever it comes from, it seems to me, something about sharing work, competition, and success makes the victory sweeter (and the loss more bearable).

One thing that makes America a great competitive society is the individuality and originality of its people. Sometimes that "rugged individualist" mentality gets in the way of partnerships. For several decades, the precepts of Frederick Taylor and others, combined with the piece-work incentive systems (like the one we had at Huffy Bicycles) worked to reinforce "pay for production" *by the individual alone.* When I arrived at the Celina, Ohio, plant, most of the people described what they did by naming the machine they ran or the type of process they operated. "I'm a press operator," or "I'm a welder," or "I work in the wheel room" was a common response. It took a concerted effort to break these people out of their "I want to depend on nobody but myself for my earnings" mentality.

Some simply refused, but the majority yielded to participating in small group, cell production and then in focused factories next. This "weaning" process was accompanied by the introduction of Improshare, Mitchell Fein's gainsharing system (on top of the direct incentive system) and later by a plantwide "base rate" replacing the direct incentive (piecework) system. The plant was really "too big" (2,000 employees) for the ideal culture and interaction, hence the decision to break it up into smaller "focused" factories. In a few years, most of the people would answer the question about what they did differently. Many would proudly say, "I am a bike builder, or I build Bicycle Parts" (one of the focused factories), or at worst, "I work in the Painted Frame and Fork factory." Ultimately, all but a few (and a few individual contributors are necessary!) became part of the new team-based partnership culture. In his recent book *The New Partnerships* [5], Tom Melohn describes it graphically, "if you take a couple drops of human dignity and respect – just a couple drops – and put them on an employee, and [if] they believe you, they'll swell up just like a sponge."

Partnering in a Learning Organization

The weaning process was accompanied by a new (revolutionary?) training process that went way beyond the TQM or employee involvement training we had done in

the mid-1980s. We called it *strategic learning* training –
for factory people. Peter Senge had written about learning
organizations in *The Fifth Discipline* [6], but his focus in
this excellent book was more on "white collar" learning.
With the help of consultant James Barber [7], we undertook to greatly enhance the involvement and flexibility of
our hourly work force (and management too!) by 12 one-
hour (each) sessions to create a learning organization in a
factory setting. After some rocky sessions, the results were
amazing. Empowerment led to original learning and
thinking. Teams began taking unheard-of initiatives.
Hourly workers traveled to supplier partners to resolve
difficult problems (such as chronic rust problems on Armco
Steel's tubing) by interacting with the supplier's hourly
workers. Armco's problem was in the process. Once diag-
nosed and implemented, the solution called for virtually
no extra cost or trouble, thanks to the interaction with the
workers.

Hourly employees usually conducted whole sections of
plant tours for customers. These workers constantly
impressed visitors with their command of the scope of the
entire business and their role in it. Hourly (union) members helped select outside consultants to redesign and
update the gainsharing plan. (Hourly employees designing
their own pay system? Yes!) The union's major problem
with all of the changes was that management would not
push the changes through fast enough. Employee to supervisor ratios approached 100 to 1 in some areas, with "team
leader-technicians" from the hourly ranks assuming many
of the traditional duties of the supervisor, but with far
more intimate knowledge of the processes. Collaboration
was rampant! Partnership was proven to be infinitely
more powerful than individual effort [8–10]. Recently
quoted in *Fortune* magazine [11], Senge confirmed what
we found back then. "People working together with
integrity and authenticity and collective intelligence are

profoundly more effective as a business than people living together based on politics, game playing, and narrow self-interest."

Another reason partnerships are a better way to success is that they provide the potential for synergy – a widely used but poorly understood word that results from the whole being much greater than the sum of the parts. Synergy is possible both within a partnership and among several partnerships. Many names have been coined to describe partnerships – alliances, joint ventures, mergers. Whatever type of legal paper is drawn up, one thing is certain: the partnership is only as good as the desire of the people entering it to make it strong, fair, and a "win-win" proposition. In the absence of these factors, legal documents provide little protection.

Create Value in the Eyes of the Customer

Finally, since this book is written from a business perspective, I will comment here, but not everywhere throughout, about two very important topics: customer value and principles. Customer value is the ultimate "scorecard" that determines who wins and who loses in business. Because it is defined in the eyes and minds of "outside" customers, partnerships can be an invaluable way to discover it (an "outside-in" process). In the last chapter, I list what I consider the attributes that combine to constitute value. A great deal of work is being done to find better ways of determining what customers really value. A very important point to remember is that customer satisfaction measures, which have been so popular, describe how customers felt about the value received only *after the fact.* What is badly needed is a way to assess what they want "now" and "in the future," even though they (the customers) often do not know themselves. How better to take the first step toward achieving this than by forming a close-knit partnership with the customers.

The Importance of Principles

The principles I refer to in the preface and in the words of noted author Stephen Covey [1] "are deep, fundamental truths. . . ." He talks of them as the "true north on a compass," not negotiable or changeable. These principles are so fundamental to institutions, associations, and organizations, not just to businesses and certainly not just to manufacturing businesses, that they warrant an entire book. (Fortunately Covey has written not one, but three fine books on various aspects of this important topic.) So much of partnering, partnerships, and relationships is based on trust, integrity, character, and principles that this chapter could not end without a reinforcement of these points, see Figure 1.1.

The Power of Partnerships was born as I reflected on what seemed to be the primary success factors in my own experience and that of other executives of successful companies whom I knew or read about. *The longer I operated major businesses, the more evident it became that my business was no better than the partnerships I could forge with suppliers, customers, associates-employees, and professional supporters. I, too, was no better than the partnerships and relationships I had built with this same group, plus one – my personal partners.* Ken Shelton [12] says, in *Executive Excellence*: "In the Old West, a partner was someone you never double-crossed – and lived to tell about it. The partnership was the one sacred relationship – not that partners don't have serious differences to reconcile."

"Magic Pills" Cure Symptoms, Not Illnesses

The more I read about all the various "magic pills," that business – especially American (impatient) businesses – searched for, an interrelationship began to emerge. A. Blanton Godfrey, chairman and CEO of the Juran Institute, said it concisely and well in a 1993

FIGURE 1.1
The Integrative Power of Partnerships

No business is better than its partners.

Choose partners carefully, you will be judged by the company you keep.

Partnerships must be built on integrity.

Conflicts must and will arise – deal with them proactively.

Make sure there is something in the partnership for both partners.

Top management commitment is essential to success.

Relationships with people are the cornerstones of partnerships.

Partnerships are the integrative next step beyond lean production, TQM, and reengineering.

Conference Board Report titled *Profiting from Total Quality* [13]. In his article "Ten Clear Trends for the Next Ten Years," he stated "One of the most exciting trends is partnering." Mr. Godfrey, I could not agree more.

Kmart chairman Joe Antonini [14] put it a little more directly: "Partnering is the survival strategy for the '90s and beyond." This is a sentiment I also share, and the sentiment extends far beyond the realm of retailing. In my experiences with Kmart, these feelings are moving through the organization but they need to move even faster and deeper. It is very difficult to change the way things have been done for years when the previous approaches have been successful. Remember Peter Drucker's sobering thought: "Whom the gods would punish, they first give 40 years of success." (OK, in Kmart's case it was only 20 years of success and then Wal*Mart came along. What Wal*Mart chairman David Glass must be wondering is who will be their nemesis!)

Four Partnerships Are the Cornerstones

As I thought about partnering, it became evident that four fundamental partnerships I have identified are the cornerstones: partnerships with *suppliers*, with *customers*, with *associates*, and *special partnerships* (with support partners, sometimes professional and often personal).

An Old Idea Whose Time Has Come

A lot has been spoken and written about the customer-supplier partnership. Former Wal*Mart executive Jack Shewmaker has been one of the most informed, credible, and outspoken advocates of this partnership – especially in the retail setting. His views over the years, and particularly stated in his 1990 remarks to the International Mass Retail Association meeting, are virtually identical to my views. I have quoted him and excerpted liberally from that 1990 speech in parts of several chapters. A more detailed quote of his is included later in this chapter for emphasis. While I genuinely agree with Jack, I believe his thoughts can be extended to a much broader application of partnership. Certainly the style of his good friend and leader Sam Walton personified partnership with Wal*Mart associates. There is much more about this tremendous example later on.

The concept of special partnerships is too often overlooked. Jack Kahl, noted CEO of Manco, the "duck" (duct) tape company, has used outside partnerships superbly in the process of building his uniquely successful company. Some of Manco and Jack's partners were "dual" in nature – Sam Walton was both a large customer-partner and an important "mentor/advisor-partner." I cited Jim Barber's help previously. The continuing intellectual partnership (consultation) with Ram Charan was a powerful influence in my successes at Huffy. The successful advertising campaigns created by Huffy's partnership with Lois USA and my cohort there Ed Holzer were also instrumental. Perhaps most of all, these three (and many others I will not name here for the sake of space) provided the most valuable help any partner can give – honest feedback, both positive and negative, but always constructive. These outside resources can provide the objective, honest "mirror" we all need badly, but only few have.

The message here is so simple it must be restated: partnerships are so powerful because they can be so diverse in type and nature. Each of these types of partnerships will be discussed in further detail in separate chapters.

Many Things Are Common to All Partnerships

Some considerations are common to all four partnerships, and those must be considered at the outset. The *choice of partners* is probably the most important consideration to start with. If the wrong partners are chosen, much effort and time will be wasted and the outcome will be far short of successful. Choosing the right partner is not easy. Someone may not want to partner with you for a variety of reasons. It is wise to choose strong partners, but if they perceive you as weak or unworthy, they may not be willing to partner with you. There are many other factors, which I will touch on as the book unfolds, to consider in this decision. Neither is it wise to delay the choice because, like many business decisions, there will never be complete information on which to base the choice. I still remember Ram Charan's admonition as he encouraged us to make sure we had the best, most cost-competitive supplier-partners in the world for our bikes, "do it, and do it fast, before the competition overtakes you."

Another of the first factors to consider is *trust*. Gather as much information as you can about your desired partner(s). Honestly list all the "issues and obstacles" that currently exist. Only by dealing with these will a genuine high-trust environment be created. Partnerships must ultimately be built on trust, but trust is hard to earn and easily lost. If you are deemed untrustworthy, you will be considered an undesirable partner. Chuck Rosner [14], president of Ekco Housewares, describes it this way, "With partnering, you build a longer term, more lasting relationship. You begin to eliminate the antagonistic attitude that has characterized [buyer-seller] relationships from time immemorial. Partnership is an attitudinal issue, a matter of trust." Because of this, the first set of qualifiers for your organization and all potential partners are based on *character and ethics*: honesty, fairness, and integrity. It is also critical that strategic partners have *common*, or at least consistent, *goals and values*.

In Figure 1.2, there is a checklist of the factors that must be present to make a successful partnership. This list is simply a quick way to recall many of the key success factors and may be useful to carry along to early discussions as a memory prompt. Add your own "factors" to this list – only you know the details and intricacies of your partnership needs. Make this growing checklist a living tool for you and your organization.

FIGURE 1.2
Checklist of Characteristics and Enhancements

_____ 1. Choice of partners

_____ 2. Willingness to become a partner

_____ 3. Trust

_____ 4. Character and ethics

_____ 5. Strategic intent

_____ 6. Culture fit

_____ 7. Consistent directions

_____ 8. Common goals and interests

_____ 9. Information sharing

_____10. Risks shared fairly

_____11. Rewards shared fairly

_____12. Resources adequately matched

_____13. Duration mutually agreed and long term

_____14. Sponsors in top management

_____15. Commitment to partnership

_____16. "Grossly similar" perceptions of the value the other brings to the partnership

_____17. Rules, policies, and performance measures support partnering

Partnering Does Not Eliminate Conflicts

Wolf Schmitt, CEO of Rubbermaid, discussing the ethics of partnership in *Executive Excellence* [15], stated: "consistent ethical behavior is essential for trust to form and grow." He maintained that business partners must achieve three things to create an ethical partnership:

1. *Clarity* – they clearly define what each expects from the other.

2. *Equity* – they define the individual benefits that each party derives through association with the other.

3. *Justice* – they agree on a place to go or a process to be followed in resolving ethical issues.

In the end, a lasting partnership cannot be driven by power, said Schmitt. It must be fueled by ethics. He concluded that "The most difficult part of partnering is negotiating and resolving the inevitable differences between partners. Achieving ethical, win-win partnerships is a continuing journey – one only we can lead."

Rules and Rewards May Inhibit Partnering

What Wolf infers in his remarks, but does not state exactly this way is that our measurements, rewards, rules,

and consequences must be aligned with partnering. Most still are not. They are still "suboptimized" rules and rewards: "Get the best price!" "Make a given gross margin!" "Turn the inventory X times!" "Stretch the terms!" Is it any surprise that operating levels of an enterprise focus on less than the "big picture"? Walter Salmon, professor of retailing and senior associate dean at Harvard Business School, commenting in *The Home Furnishings Periodical* (HFD) [14] states, "much more needs to be done to modify organizations and incentive systems to maximize the potential of partnerships. . . ."

The associates are rewarded for what they do (or perhaps, more significantly, punished and fired for what they do not do!). The often repeated but still ignored phrase "What gets measured gets done!" seems to ring in my ears. We must define new partnership-based measures that reward performance through partnering with the entire core business system in mind. (The concept of *core business systems* or "suprasystems" optimizes the entire system to achieve a business purpose. Defined in depth by G. Harland Carothers and his associates [16], it is a concept that is totally integrative and complimentary to the partnerships as described here.)

There Has to Be Enough in It for Both Partners

The concepts of a *mutual self-interest* (benefit) and a level of *shared risk* are also fundamental to building a partnership. This will be discussed in more detail in the chapters that follow, because the relative levels of "need" and risk determine the importance of the partnership to those involved. Ideally, the levels are similar enough that both partners will benefit substantially, making the partnership a win-win proposition. However, even though this concept seems obviously good for both parties and should be easy to achieve, it is not. Jack Kahl, CEO of Manco, commenting in his newsletter *Duck Tales* [17], says it another way: "Said easily. Accomplished with a great deal of difficulty. Building a win-win partnership often seems like trying to nail Jell-O to a wall."

A Culture Match Is Like a Blood-Type Match

Are the cultures of the two partners compatible? Since a partnership in its ideal state is a close working relationship, a "culture match" is very important. When cultures (loosely defined as "the way we do things around here") do not match, it is much more likely that disputes will arise over the way interaction occurs, even if there is strong agreement about the desire for the partnership to succeed. The culture of the partners usually is a reflection of deeply held beliefs and customs. It is often a good barometer of the character of the organizations as well. Because of this, a culture match, like a blood-type match in a medical sense, should be done early in the partnership effort. This can head off a lot of wasted time and frustration. It can also warn of impending problems long before they otherwise surface. The concept is particularly important when the potential partners are of two widely different *geographical cultures.*

In my experience with the bicycle industry, far more bicycles are made and sold outside the United States (by almost 10 to 1) than in it. Most of the bicycle component industry also resides in either Europe or Asia (although the recent weakening of the dollar has caused a resurgence in both U.S. bike and component producers). In spite of this, most Americans are surprised to learn that many of the best new innovative ideas in bicycles and components were discovered while attending major expositions in Italy, Germany, Japan, or Taiwan. Just as good ideas come from all over the world, the "rules" of doing business, both written and unwritten, vary widely from country to country and continent to continent. Since multinational ownership of companies is now common, it is important to know the culture of the owner or parent of a potential partner, otherwise some untimely surprises could spring up.

Win-Win Is Best, Principled Negotiations Help

Even in the best partnerships, differences will arise. If the partners can evolve to "principled negotiations" about these differences, the resolution will be easier and the tone of the partnership better. The book *Getting to Yes* by Fisher and Ury of the Harvard Negotiation Project [18] gives a good description of the process of a principled negotiation. In this process, a negotiation system is worked out based on factual information, principles, or other less emotional or debatable factors. Reaching agreement is facilitated by virtue of having the stability of some "agreed upon" facts, principles, or benchmarks. I did not say it was easy, just easier than the other ways. Stephen Covey also states one of his seven habits as "Think Win-Win." Notice he says *think* ahead of *win-win*. He knows a win-win agreement may not always be possible. (Some participants may not care about or want a win-win, as long as they win!) It is important to try finding this out early. When using a book for the learning process, it is best if all partners have read it. If not, the result could be similar to the story about the two hunters who had used up all their ammunition in lion country, then encountered an angry lion. One hunter tells the other, "I've read all about this situation. The books say we should look the lion right in the eye, and he will leave us alone." The other hunter's reply was, "I know. I've read the book, and you've read the book, but has the lion read the book?" This happened to me. Once, shortly after reading *Getting to Yes*, I was scheduled to visit a large customer to discuss a delicate pricing problem. I went fully prepared to engage in a principled negotiation and "get to yes." Unfortunately, the customer's people had been schooled in the win-lose negotiation approach and soundly thrashed me. The only principle they were interested in was "getting their way." They had not read the same book I had!

Elephants and Mice Can Live Together

Elephants and mice can live together, but only if elephants watch their step and mice move quickly. Once past this major hurdle, other issues come up. Is this a partner whose goals are congruent with yours (or at least compatible)? Are the *size and scope* of the partners such that the partnership will be important to both? For a very small company to partner with a very large one is often perilous (for the small one) unless what it provides in the partnership is of significant value to the larger partner. Many small suppliers that gained Wal*Mart's business learned about this kind of problem – painfully.

Aspirations Should Be in the Same Universe

If the strategic intent [19] of one of the partners is (global?) market leadership or dominance in any respect, do the other potential partners share that lofty ambition? (They should!) If the levels of ambition are greatly different, the partners will likely have difficulties agreeing on the definition of success and amount of investment appropriate. (The term *investment* is intended to include capital and people or time.) If one partner relaxes after seizing a given (home) country or continent market while the other aspires to dominance throughout a major sphere of market influence, such as North America, Europe, or the Pacific Rim, the partnership is certain to be strained or damaged beyond repair. Similarly, in this example, the *relative resources* of the two partners must be considered since one may require more than the other can invest in either capital or personnel.

The Power Balance in Partnerships

When one of the partners has some form of power over the other, this power must be very carefully controlled or the partnership will turn into the cliché that makes *partnership* the most overused and abused word in business relationships. Some of these power sensitive partnerships are employer-employee, buyer-seller, and parent-child. The balance of power in the partnership influences the tone of the relationship and is an important factor to consider at the outset. A single personality-centered power broker can inhibit partnering for years if not neutralized. "But how do I do that?" is the most commonly asked question. "If I go over the buyer's head, I may never get any business in the future." There is a delicate art to going over a buyer's head – a little like juggling bottles of nitro-glycerine or chain saws. The best approach is to do it with the individual's consent and help. Talk of the *need* for your senior management to meet theirs and request that person's help to set up the meeting and be involved. Another way is to say that your boss insists on meeting with their boss – assuming you have determined that this is so! However you achieve this multilevel contact, it is a must!

Be Patient and Persistent in Your Pursuit

Once some meetings have occurred, be patiently persistent. One way to think of it is "you do not expect to get married after the first date – just get another date." Even if the partnership begins on a very short-term basis, do it! The *duration* of the partnership can be gradually extended as trust and cooperation are developed. It is entirely acceptable to enter a partnership for a limited time (a year or season) to get started. The important thing is to get started and then refine the relationship as it builds. An old associate of mine used to say, "Postponed perfection is the enemy of planned progress." (This is a good phrase to remember for many things.)

Commitment at the Top Is Essential

Another very important condition of any partnership, if it is to be a long-term, successful one, is the sponsorship and support of the top person (or people): executives, owners, directors, managers, or whoever they are. Without that support, sponsorship, and active involvement, the partnership cannot achieve the full success possible and will likely fail. The first serious trouble could tear the partnership apart. In the chapters that discuss each of the basic partnerships, we will explore where the partnership is best originated, if it is to have the best chance of success.

Good Partnerships Are Like Good Customers

In a 1991 survey conducted in the United States by the Association for Manufacturing Excellence [20], a number of characteristics of what defined a good customer were ranked in importance. These characteristics were very similar to what defines a good partnership (since the supplier-customer combination encompasses two of the four partnership legs). Even though technology and negotiation were ranked low in importance, the most telling point was what types of factors ranked high. Relationship-based factors and process-based factors were rated the most important. Also evident in the responses were strong feelings about trust builders and destroyers.

Some of the *trust builders* were

- Open, honest, timely communication
- Involvement and participation
- Objective feedback and constructive criticism
- Sharing strategic direction
- Multi-year agreements when justified.

The *trust destroyers* were often based on behaviors that did not match discussions (not "walking the talk"):

- Unreasonable demands and one-way communication
- Talking about quality and service and then buying on price alone
- Decisions made by (higher) authorities not involved with the partnership
- Leveraging one supplier against the other
- Basing business on price only, not total value.

A few basic commitments are necessary to build a successful strategic partnership. Bob Rockey [21], president of Levi Strauss of North America, describes five:

1. Dedication to a consumer-focused business approach

2. A common goal of driving unnecessary costs from both sides

3. Support and buy-in for each other's visions and strategies

4. An integral role in each other's success

5. Commitment to breaking down barriers to shared information.

It becomes clear from those who have successfully built and participated in strategic partnerships that four of the "co" words are keys to success: commitment, collaboration, communication, and cooperation. To quote Rockey: "We view these relationships as a requirement of doing business. We are seeing them pay off for both parties every day. Maximizing the opportunities presented by these alliances will position us for success as we move into the twenty-first century."

The Next Step Beyond Reengineering

Writing in the Index SMI Review in late 1993 [22], James Champy, coauthor (with Michael Hammer) of the hugely successful and widely applied Reengineering the Corporation, discussed "What comes after reengineering?" In answer to the question "What areas are particularly fertile?" (to explore for what comes next) – he replied: "One topic area we find interesting is the extended organization. New models of organization suggest extended relationships with partners – customers, suppliers, and so forth. What, in fact, do they look like?" The answer is they look like as many different faces as the universe of situations demand, but they are all built around the same framework – strong partnerships with a few key stakeholders or constituents.

In the same answer, Champy's colleague Robert Morrison talked about studies being considered by their firm, CSC Index: "Naturally we think two topics for 1994 are particularly important: 'the strategically structured corporation' and 'managing the reengineered corporation.' The first is a study of how companies can organize themselves, forge alliances, and insource or outsource processes to promote their strategic intent. The second is an investigation into the emerging roles and responsibilities of senior managers. This is an area where not much work has been done."

The Next Step Beyond Lean Production

The concept of partnerships is not a new one. In a 1990 pamphlet on partnership, CIBA-Geigy stated: "Long-term growth and profitability can be mutually achieved by partnerships between customers and suppliers. . . . These arrangements often prove to be the most efficient means of problem solving because of improved communication, understanding and mutual commitment." In fact, this topic is new only in the expanded context in which it is proposed in this book. Others are realizing the extent to which this new context provides a framework for competing in the 1990s and beyond. In the March–April 1994 *Harvard Business Review* lead article, James Womack and Daniel Jones [23] also explored for the next steps. Their book *The Machine That Changed The World* introduced the concept of lean production and described how it changed the competitive balance in worldwide automobile manufacturing. They write, "We've seen numerous examples of amazing improvements in a specific activity in a single company. But these experiences have also made us realize that applying lean production techniques to discrete activities is not the end of the road. If individual breakthroughs can be linked up and down the value chain to form a continuous value stream that creates, sells, and services a family of products, the performance of the whole can be raised to a dramatically higher level." This is the essence of the power of partnerships in its ideal use.

They continue by stating, "We think that value-creating activities can be joined, but this effort will require a new organizational model: the lean enterprise. As we envision it, the lean enterprise is a group of individuals, functions, and legally separate but operationally synchronized companies. The notion of the value stream defines the lean enterprise."

Whether it is, in fact, "the next step after reengineering" or the creation of "the lean enterprise" matters only in the name it is called. The essence of what *it* is continues to be the partnership between a manufacturer, suppliers, customers, associates-employees, and external support partners. The formation and mastery of these partnerships create an immense competitive power – the power of customer value maximization.

Partnerships Enable and Integrate Agility

There are so many reasons for partnering step, I am unable to chronicle all of them. In fact, every week I find several more. One that I would like to touch on briefly is the recently emerged concepts of agility and the virtual corporation. (I have heard about so many "virtual" things lately, I wonder if the next step will be to sell virtual products and services for which people will pay with virtual money!) The concept of agility does have merit. Lehigh University's Iacocca Institute has now formed an Agility Forum to capture and refine all of the potential uses. In reading several of their "white papers," I was pleased to find many of their conclusions and directions totally in line with partnerships. I believe that agility, like leanness and many of the other similar concepts, are of vital importance but deal with only part of the enterprise.

Only the core business systems (suprasystems) and partnerships are integrative and dynamic enough to span the entire business enterprise. The Agility Forum's papers constantly reference topics [24] such as "interactive supplier-customer relationships, leveraging resources through cooperation, win-win alliances, the power of cooperation, inter-enterprise teaming, and the value of sharing information." *This sounds like partnering to me!* They speak often about the need for a "new kind of social contract between employer and employee" to "maximize human initiative." Refer to Chapter 4 and form your own opinion. The agility experts' viewpoint starts with manufacturing and quickly evolves to an enterprise-wide view. Their initial "position paper" [25] is a joint industry led effort and states: "the agile manufacturing enterprise develops strategic relationships with its consumer, as well as . . . customers." It continues, "An agile enterprise has the organizational flexibility to adopt . . . the managerial vehicle that will yield the greatest competitive advantage. Sometimes it will take the form of collaborative ventures with other companies, and sometimes it will take the form of a virtual company."

In a recent *Industry Week* article entitled "Back to the Future, Revisiting the Promise of the Virtual Corporation" [26], Roger Nagel of the Iacocca Institute comments at some length on how partnerships can create what is now referred to as the *virtual corporation*. "I want to have a group of people willing to partner with us because . . . we can trust each other, we have common business objectives, and we are compatible on the cultural and organizational [levels]. . . ." He continues, "While some companies might insist partnerships be etched out legally, the 'virtual' assemblage favors loose alliances of suppliers and manufacturers. In demanding strict alliances, companies have complicated the virtual corporation's most outstanding competitive strength – simplicity."

Consider this with the content of Chapter 6 and see if the views of Nagel and the agility proponents do not embrace partnership formation as the essential cornerstone step to "virtuality" (whatever that means). In the same article, Jordan Lewis, author of the book *Partnerships for Profit: Structuring and Managing Strategic Alliances,* clarifies his position [27]. "I used to teach about market-entry barriers at Wharton, and I was dead wrong. Alliances and partnerships change the game overnight." He goes on, "companies must partner or perish. But defensively backing into partnerships could prove a transparent solution."

Partnerships Are Special Relationships

Finally, let's return to Walter Salmon's description of how partnerships differ from traditional relationships [14]:

- They are enduring rather than episodic.
- They are multifunctional rather than only buyer-seller.
- They are based on the rapid and complete exchange of what was previously considered confidential data.

He adds, "Progress has been substantial, but we've barely scratched the potential improvement opportunities that may arise from partnership."

Assess What You Have (or Want) Right Now

The assessment format shown in Figure 1.3 in the following pages should be used to evaluate both current and potential partnerships for likelihood of success. For current ones it is a diagnostic tool. For potential ones, it is a refined form of the checklist shown in Figure 1.2. The health and effectiveness of those partnerships can be measurably improved by considering all the ingredients of a successful partnership. If both partners complete such an assessment, it can provide valuable feedback and generate dialogue. Each partner is likely to have a somewhat biased view of what is "fair." Do not let this impede progress – it is to be expected. If the score is below 50, there is a problem with the partnership, probably one that is limiting its effectiveness. If the score is over 70, the partnership should be humming along, producing good results for both partners. Under 30, it really is no partnership, just some kind of relationship that has been masquerading as a partnership, misleading everyone. I have inserted this assessment in an early stage to provide a "learning tool" for wider application later. Do not spend too much time agonizing over the rating the first time through – just do it! As more assessments are done, the meaning of each of the 17 items will take on a context relevant to the person doing the assessment.

Sometimes It Just Will Not Work

Occasionally, in spite of the best efforts, persistence, and a lot of work, a partnership goes sour. It just stops working. In those cases, the assessment will probably confirm your "gut feeling." The partnership is over. When that happens, assess what went wrong as best you can and drop back to an arm's length relationship. I do not believe in "burning bridges," but continuing to behave as if a dysfunctional partnership is working is a license to fail. Just as in the marriage example earlier, sometimes things just do not work out. Act quickly once the recognition is clear. There are more productive places to devote that time and energy than in a failed partnership.

Having considered several of these universal partnership criteria, it is now time to consider in more depth the specifics of the four primary partnerships: with suppliers, customers, associates, and supporters. The next chapters will be written from the perspective of a central position, looking outward to the four "compass points" at the partnerships situated on each.

FIGURE 1.3
Assesment of Partnership Potential for Success

Rate from   1 = very poor
              2 = somewhat poor
              3 = average
              4 = somewhat good
              5 = very good

Circle One

1. **Choice of partners**   1 2 3 4 5
   (Is this a strategically valuable partner for your business?)

2. **Willingness to become a partner** 1 2 3 4 5
   (Does this partner desire to become your partner?)

3. **Trust**   1 2 3 4 5
   (Is there a good level of trust or the possibility of one?)

4. **Character and ethics**   1 2 3 4 5
   (Has experience proven this exists or can exist?)

5. **Strategic intent**   1 2 3 4 5
   (Do the aspirations of both partners match or are they compatible?)

6. **Culture fit**   1 2 3 4 5
   (Do the partners have similar or compatible cultures?)

7. **Consistent directions**   1 2 3 4 5
   (Is there a consistent direction for partnering efforts – on both parties' behalf?)

8. **Common goals and interests** 1 2 3 4 5
   (Are the goals and interests of the partners shared fairly equally?)

9. **Information sharing**   1 2 3 4 5
   (Can both partners feel good about liberal information sharing?)

continued

FIGURE 1.3 (*CONT'D*)

Rate from   1 = very poor
              2 = somewhat poor
              3 = average
              4 = somewhat good
              5 = very good

Circle One

10. Risks shared fairly   1   2   3   4   5
(Are the risks to both partners fairly equal?)

11. Rewards shared fairly   1   2   3   4   5
(Are the rewards and potential gains for both partners fairly equal?)

12. Resources adequately matched   1   2   3   4   5
(Does the smaller partner have adequate resources to support the larger?)

13. Duration mutually agreed long term 1   2   3   4   5
(Do the partners agree on a long-term partnership?)

14. Sponsors in top management of both 1   2   3   4   5
(Is there good top management support at both partners?)

15. Commitment to partnership by both 1   2   3   4   5
(Is there a fairly broad level of commitment by both partners?)

16. Value given and received   1   2   3   4   5
(Do both partners have "grossly similar" perceptions of the value the other brings to the partnership?)

17. Rules, policies, and measures   1   2   3   4   5
(Do these key measures reinforce the desired partnership behavior?)

Total Score: _____

Chapter 2

Partnerships with Suppliers

KEY POINTS

- Good suppliers are essential to a good business.
- A fair deal is one where you would take either side.
- What goes around, comes around.
- "There ain't no such thing as a free lunch."
- If they will do it for you, they might do it to you.
- The truth will set you free, but you may suffer from it.
- Get competitive or get lost.
- Top down + bottom up = strong partnerships.
- Lip service just will not cut it – walk the talk.
- Trust is the basis – sharing information is the proof.
- You are your supplier's agent.

Unless someone can figure out how to defy the laws of physics, and "make something from nothing," suppliers are an essential part of any business. Whether the suppliers provide goods and/or services, they play a pivotal role in your success. When external conditions change and a reconfiguration of the business is needed to retain (or gain, or capitalize on) a competitive advantage, this is possible only if the linkage (partnership?) with high-quality suppliers makes it possible. If the linkage is weak, the supplier will not or cannot respond. If the supplier is not a high-quality supplier, the supplier's response would not be sufficient. In either case – you lose!

Abused Suppliers Should Be Wary

How ironic, in this enlightened context of suppliers' importance, is it that so many times suppliers are used and abused. I can remember the training I received at my first job involving suppliers. The suppliers were adversaries, often almost enemies. The challenge was to outwit them, and if you could not outsmart them, then bully them into submission whenever and however possible. A decade ago, a business associate of mine told me his purchasing philosophy: "keep the suppliers on the defensive and perilously perched on the precipice of bankruptcy – without pushing them over the edge." Another described the proper philosophy as "getting the last ounce of blood out of them." Later in my career, I felt the other side of this unpleasant relationship, when as a seller, I had to cope with customers who were trying to do to me just what I had been trained to do to my suppliers. It was miserable – but it was the way things were and unfortunately still are, beneath the superficial "partnership" claims, in too many business relationships.

To counter this attitude, suppliers charged "what the market would bear" and often pocketed a handsome profit, even if it made their customers noncompetitive. Whoever could take advantage of the other did so. (Sounds like a great basis for a working relationship.) John Guaspari, writing in Rath & Strong's *Leadership Report* [28], uses an example of "old-style" counterproductive behavior: "consider the case of a plant manager and a sales rep. .... The plant manager was very busy and wants to spend as little time as possible talking to peddlers. 'All they're interested in is pushing product, . . . so I give five minutes.' What is the sales rep going to do with his five minutes? Push product, that's what."

Only suppliers who had a legacy of making top quality products continued to do so – and not even all of them. During the consumption-oriented times of the 1960s and 1970s, abusing suppliers and adversary relations were the norm. So was poor quality in the "good enough" mentality. Only suppliers who had built their reputations on superior quality were prone to continue with it, and as competitive pressures mounted, they too fell prey to cost reduction at the expense of quality. I can still recall a question posed to me by one of our (start-up) factory employees in 1980: "Do you want us to make it fast or make it right?" The answer to both was, of course, "yes." Suppliers squeezed to the last ounce of blood certainly felt similarly, and they often made it fast and just barely good enough (most of the time). Fortunately for all of us, some companies believed so strongly in doing what was right that they held fast to making high-quality material in spite of intense competitive price pressure applied by astute purchasing agents.

Adversary Treatment = Adversary Reaction

The arm's length, adversary relationship reinforces exactly the wrong (adversary) behavior. No positive outcome is likely until this loop of adversary relations can be broken. Something must change – and someone must go first! Since the only behavior you can control is your own – the change needs to come from you. Yet, as recently as late 1992, "Inaki" Lopez of GM was believed to be doing the same thing, wrapped in the jargon of his PICOS program, "warrior" diet, and related hype. I spoke with him during that time, and I do not know how much he genuinely intended to "brutalize" the GM supplier network. He claimed he simply saw few alternatives to such a harsh wake-up call. He believed the future of the U.S. auto industry, and especially GM, was at stake, but no one took the consequences seriously enough. His purchasing approach had been hugely successful in Europe, so why not transplant it to the United States? "Get competitive or get out" is certainly a valid position, but it fails to consider one of the most powerful aspects of partnership-based supplier relations – good, cooperative design. The legacy he left with his behavior may have enhanced short-term profits but damaged supplier relations, and long-term profits.

The ability to be competitive is dependent on producing materials, components, and assemblies to a design that is, in itself, inherently competitive and doing so with the cooperation of the creator of that design. A recent *Business Week* update on the GM supplier situation in the article "Hardball is still GM's game," quotes these feelings [29]: "We're not gonna bust our fanny for (GM) anymore," and "There is an anger out there that's palpable." Further explanation cites GM's practice of frequent quoting and requoting on contracts "makes it difficult for us to plan people, capacity, and equipment more than a year ahead." The article goes on, "Suppliers agree, however, that GM's purchasing staff is no longer as abrasive as during Lopez' tenure." This sounds to me like faint praise – you can form your own opinion. I have known a lot of fine people who work for GM, so the issue is not whether GM is "bad." The issue is one of damaged trust. The closing sentence bears this out: "Lopez may be gone, they say, but his ghost will haunt GM for years to come."

How much incentive do you suppose there was for suppliers to really cooperate in the design stage or concentrate on superb quality or delivery when they were constantly on the defensive, protecting themselves, and trying to make a profit? Simply threatening or bullying suppliers works in the short term. It fails over the long term because they either "get even" or just direct their best efforts to competing customers who are better partners. In the book *The Machine that Changed the World* [30], there is an excellent description of how supplier relations should operate in a lean production environment. This environment is a good comparison to a good, effective supplier partnership. For that reason, I will not go too deeply into the topic, but focus on what is not described there: how to start, build, and "enjoy" a partnership that makes "lean" operating principles possible to apply.

Partners Stick Together in Good or Bad Times

During the early 1970s in the United States most industrial commodities were in very short supply and supplier relations' leverage took a turn for the suppliers. Supplier relationships took on a whole new meaning, for a while at least. Manufacturers had to be much more creative and they had to hope that those suppliers over whom they had used leverage for many years would not treat them the same way now that the leverage had shifted to the suppliers' hands. Manufacturers who had been "fair" with their suppliers were repaid with enough material to reasonably support their production needs. After a year of this condition, things returned pretty much to normal. Purchasers continued to claim that these were still partnerships, but to them that resumed meaning "you give and we take." This could have been a worthwhile learning experience, but it too passed. It yielded to a recovery in the late 1970s, in which the buyers once again wielded the "big pencil" and the heavy hand.

JIT: One of the First "Magic Pills"

About that time something called JIT started emerging as a management buzzword. In typical adversary fashion, buyers interpreted JIT with meaning, "transfer the inventory responsibility to the suppliers and make them hold it and deliver it *just in time*." Instead of the real benefits of JIT (which most people now realize were higher quality and reduced costs through less total inventory), the benefit might have accrued temporarily to the buyer. Eventually the cost of carrying the inventory and, in fact, the uncertainty about what inventory to carry (since it was one step further from the point of use), actually did not lower costs but led to higher costs.

This misuse of JIT translated into either higher prices or further weakening of the supplier. In place of the benefits of JIT, what occurred in most cases was a shift in the inventory carrying costs from purchaser to supplier. The accumulation of inventory was moved one step further from the point of sale, actually increasing the errors inherent in forecasts and adding further to costs. This translated into either higher prices (needed) or reduced profitability (for the suppliers). Only in the 1980s, when enlightened managers realized the error in this process, did remedial action begin.

For the vast majority of companies the realization of the suppliers' importance as a partner in the business began to emerge only in the 1980s. As foreign (mostly Orient-based) competition with low-cost labor began taking more and more business from American companies, American manufacturers worked to drive down their labor (and related overhead) costs. This elevated purchased materials to an ever increasing percentage of the cost and sales dollar. Somewhere along the line astute managers realized that, with purchased materials ranging from 50–75 percent of every dollar of cost or sales, they might want to treat these suppliers with a little more respect and perhaps even treat them like the partners that they deserved to be.

In fact, the growth of highly competent and demanding retailers like Wal*Mart actually continue the inventory pressure on suppliers who cannot react to the ever shorter shipping windows (three days on most items and as little as one day on some).

Supplier Importance Grows With Cost Pressure

Another series of events, happening concurrently in the 1980s, underscored the importance of supplier relationships. The U.S. dollar strengthened significantly, putting extreme pressure on U.S. manufacturers to reduce costs (or join the exodus of producers to the low-wage countries of the Pacific Rim). As U.S. manufacturers fought to lower their labor costs (since cheap labor was the major advantage of Orient producers), something interesting happened – purchased material became, by far, the largest component of cost. Only when material passed the 50 percent of cost (or of sales) level and domestic suppliers dropped like flies did many top purchasing executives realize the importance of the supplier networks. Ironically, the department store industry, a long predecessor to the discount stores, referred to their suppliers as "resources," but sadly, seldom treated them that way.

In his 1990 speech, Shewmaker "confesses" to continuing this trend while he was at Wal*Mart [31]:

> When looking back at these relationships, and I must say I have been a part of the conflict just the same as most of you. I think retailer emphasis was on gaining the upper-hand or, putting it in my terminology, "one-upmanship." We made suppliers compete one against the other with frequent changes which were based on reasons that were often poorly supported by fact, or even circumstance.

As the concept of partnership with suppliers grew in obvious importance, a number of significant ways of developing that partnership began to emerge.

First of all, customers started sharing their strategic and operational plans with suppliers. Instead of keeping suppliers in the dark and throwing orders "over the wall" to them, customers actually began to communicate, to share information, and to even share future planning with the suppliers. McDonald's, the leader in the worldwide fast-food industry, was also one of the leaders in partnerships with suppliers. Many of the current leaders learned from McDonald's. However, McDonald's suppliers are unique to begin with. Many of them have open-book relationships and McDonald's is their only customer. In spite of the risk of such an arrangement, they have no contract. Companies like Martin-Brower have grown from small operations to half-billion dollar concerns based solely on McDonald's [32].

For many, however, this was not possible before going through an even more important first step – selecting the key suppliers to work with and reducing the total number of available future partners. McDonald's is a classic example of a company that attracts lots of potential partners but has a difficult task sorting out those to deal with. This is, perhaps, the single most important step in the partnership with suppliers.

Beauty May Be Only Skin Deep, but Ugliness Goes to the Bone!

No partnership effort can turn a really bad supplier into a good supplier. The selection process and the screening leading to that selection are absolutely critical. The process that cannot be done simply by a buyer or even by the purchasing function alone. It must go all the way to include the top management of both organizations. It must be clear that the management philosophies, styles, and structures of the supplier partner are compatible with those of the customer. Just to gather enough information to intelligently make such a selection is a time-consuming process. The process involves in-depth reviews by teams of purchasing, quality, engineering, and senior management. It is critical to understand all aspects of the supplier's business and operating methods. If there is no reasonably good relationship to start with, often a supplier will not feel good enough about a customer to divulge all this information in the fear that it will somehow be used against that firm with competing suppliers (reminiscent of the 1960s and 1970s). In some cases, the safest way to select a partner is to ask one of your current top performing partners to expand into a new area and become a supplier-partner in that area, too.

You May Be Judged by the Company You Keep

No matter how good a company is, if its people do a poor job of selecting suppliers and ends up with weak or underdeveloped suppliers, its progress will be slowed if not stopped. In fact, picking the wrong suppliers in too many instances can actually cause the company to fail. Picking the right ones, however, will speed progress. Shewmaker also underscores this point.

> Probably a development of greater significance than the advancement of technology is concrete evidence that suppliers and retailers who have developed effective partnership programs are progressing more rapidly than others. The idea that a supplier is thrown out or chastised the minute they don't agree to retailer programs, or the minute they make a mistake, is not in keeping with today's new management philosophy.

Know What You Want, You May Get It

It is difficult to decide whether the supplier's business objectives and operating methods are compatible until you have thoroughly analyzed and fully defined your own. How do you really want to operate? What is your strategic plan and is it clear? Do you have a clear mission or vision? Can it be written down concisely so that you can communicate it to suppliers? They need to know it.

> Perhaps most important, can you do your share and make the change into the risky behavior of trusting a supplier (or customer) that for years you have distrusted? The whole issue of trust is critical and underlies every chapter, every type of partnership. Two specific areas of importance merit further discussion in partnerships with suppliers. The first is supplier development and the second is supplier scheduling (information sharing).

Help Supplier Partners Succeed

It is amazing how many companies have large staffs of engineers, quality control people, and support staff for their factories yet expect a few people in the purchasing department to perform all the comparable activities with a supplier base that may supply three to four times the value of factory content, coming from 10 to 50 times the number of locations. This is an obvious inequity in resource allocation. It is critical that engineering, quality, and purchasing functions work as a team with the marketing and manufacturing "customers" who use the purchased materials to develop the suppliers. They must do this just as they would work to develop an internal department or work center.

The initial selection of the suppliers to be developed depends (as referenced earlier) on the selection of the critical suppliers for the long-term future. Once this has been done, development teams can begin planning and making visits to the supplier. During these visits, they must survey the supplier's current situation and create evaluations with suitable development plans (for areas of weakness). Such plans provide the basis for positive dialogue and constructive improvement for the supplier.

Obviously, the goal is for the supplier to deliver cost-competitive materials of the desired quality on a very timely basis. Suppliers can do this only if they, themselves, are competent in all three areas: cost competitiveness, quality systems, and delivery support systems (planning, control, etc.). They can also live up to customer's expectations only if those expectations are clearly communicated and understood. Japanese auto companies like Honda America are reportedly very demanding of suppliers. They do, however, usually consider their responsibility in the partnership when things get very tough. In a quote from an *Industry Week* article, a Japanese purchasing manager at Honda answers a subordinate's proposal to switch sources this way: "Wait a minute. Have we at

Honda done everything we possibly can do to make this supplier successful?" If only it happened this way most of the time. (In my experience, it rarely does!)

This is why many leading companies today are developing supplier manuals and keeping them up to date with all of their latest and most accurate expectations (beyond the data contained on the blueprint or purchase order). A very strong supplier development program will involve everything from surveys and evaluations to actual training presented or performed by the customer at the supplier's location, Mutual visits help to better understand requirements and diagnose problems. Continued reviews of progress and development of future plans on a joint basis solidify the partnership.

Learn from Suppliers, and Both Benefit

One unexpected fortunate result from the supplier development process is that the survey team learns better methods, and processes from the supplier. These improved approaches can be brought "home" for use in the customer's business. They also provide the survey teams with cumulative learning similar to best practices benchmarking. As time goes on, rotating the survey team members (one at a time or alternating teams) becomes a development process for your own people.

Another important process in developing partnerships with suppliers is that of *supplier scheduling*. Supplier scheduling is possible only if the supplier has attained a sufficient degree of competence (to deliver good quality on a timely basis). This process involves making the supplier an extension of your own company, plant, or department by the open sharing of information. The output of materials resource planning (MRP), or whatever your planning and scheduling process is called, is downloaded from the computer screen or hard copy directly to the supplier. (Wal*Mart shares a tie-in to something they call *Retail Link*, which provides up-to-date retail sales activity on all the items supplied. This is the predecessor to "demand" in their process.) After a planner or scheduler (or buyer, etc.) has reviewed the most recent information and made the appropriate delivery changes, the information is transmitted directly to the supplier.

Get Hooked Up – However You Can

Do not get hung up on Technology, start with a simple method. The process of supplier scheduling is most effective when it replaces traditional hard copy purchase orders. Obviously, if an electronic data interchange (EDI) linkage exists, it can be used. Many times the cost or complexity of developing compatible EDI links is a concern, especially for small suppliers or customers. Most have faxes and are less intimidated by this step, because it is more like what they are used to. (EDI can readily follow when the information systems linkage and working processes are in place and proven.)

In a typical product business, the data is usually organized in part number or product (category) sequence, with a line or two devoted to the information for each required delivery. The list starts with the current or past due deliveries and extends into the future as far as the planning horizon dictates. "Lines" that are "firm purchase orders" are denoted by a (symbol or letter) code prominently displayed (usually at the right or left end of the line). These are previously agreed upon as legally binding orders to be delivered.

The next chronological group of "lines" are "projections." These are production plans for which the supplier has assurance that the material purchased to produce them will be consumed by the customer (somehow, sometime) if requirements change and firm orders do not result as shown on the plans.

The last group is denoted as "forecasts," which are nonbinding but provide visibility of plans expected for the future. This visibility allows the supplier to anticipate and plan for such things as capacity problems, seasonal disruptions (such as vacation shutdowns), and opportunities for economically desirable quantity purchases or runs. Sometimes this information alone triggers discussions that either avoid problems or save money or both.

Since all plans change constantly, another "highlight" code must flag those changes for the supplier's attention. (While this sounds like a lot of detailed description, often just getting started is the largest obstacle. Now there is no mystery.)

This process, when used properly with qualified suppliers, is a very effective one. The equivalent in the retailing field is often referred to as *vendor managed inventory* or *replenishment* (VMI or VMR). This is an essential part of a quick response (QR) partnership and a concept often referred to as *category management*. Another acronym to mention is Efficient Consumer Response (ECR). These processes usually are driven by retail point-of-sale information (like Wal*Mart's Retail Link), which allows both the retailer and supplier to monitor consumer demand. Knowing what is "in the pipeline" due to shipments, what is on-hand inventory (not always available or reliable), and what are consumers' purchases provide essential pieces of information. These permit revisions to forecasts and production plans to support volatile demands on shorter lead times than would otherwise be possible.

Lest we digress too far on this one aspect of the partnership, let's return to the development of the entire partnership.

Beware People Who Do Not "Walk the Talk"

During the 1980s, in varying degrees and timing, the concept of partnerships with suppliers continued to emerge as a part of the business's strategy. As in all cases, a few companies were ahead of the movement by the foresight of their founders or executives, but most came around slowly. Habits built over the years die hard. Even when top executives recognized and championed "partnerships," the execution in the purchasing ranks changed only a little. The "dictators became more benevolent" is the way one colleague put it. Numerous irritants inhibited this relationship. Since my experience over the past 15 years has been mostly as a supplier to large retailers, I will use a list of irritants derived from that type of partnership. This list will be repeated in the chapter on customer partnerships because the irritants are the same — just viewed from the opposite direction. Many of these will be identical whether the customer-supplier types or industries remain the same or change totally.

Key Irritants from the Customer's Viewpoint:

- Stockouts, late delivery or poor quality.

- Backorders and long reorder cycles.

- Inadequate communication or poor information.

- Confusing or rapidly changing terms and allowances.

- Unrelated or unclear marketing campaigns.

- Frequent personnel changes in sales representatives or account managers.

- Incomplete or poorly thought-out promotions and plans.

- Inadequate lead times on promotion plans.

- Inaccessibility to supplier management.

- Inexplicable policies (at least by the sales representatives).

- Billing disagreements.

- New product introductions or major product line changes with short or no advance notice.

- Decentralized and often autonomous multiple division structures where sales representatives from the same company sell closely related but different products to the same buyer, with differing terms, programs, and so on.

Key Irritants from the Supplier's Viewpoint:

- Confusing or complicated scheduling of appointments and meetings with buyers.

- Buying decisions attributed to anonymous sources such as "the committee" or simply "they."

- Execution of delivery, setup, installation, display, or promotion different from what was agreed upon.

- Sudden changes in inventory needs – cutbacks or cancellations or unexpected surges in demand – with little or no advance notice.

- Failure to keep planned meeting schedules or allowing meetings to be delayed inexplicably for hours.

- Sudden or major strategic direction or product specification changes.

- Last minute cancellation of promotions that had been organized at great expense and for which inventory has already been committed.

- Frequent buying staff changes or changes in the mix of assigned duties.

- Inaccessible senior management.

- Billing disputes and deductions.

How to Partner for Competitive Advantage

Against this backdrop of historical precedent, let's explore both the benefits (which are now more widely known and accepted) and the process of building a true, effective partnership with a group of critical suppliers. The partnerships with a set of suppliers strategically aligned with the critical purchases (and purposes!) of the manufacturer yield the greatest competitive advantages and benefits. I use an example I am familiar with to illustrate.

In the bicycle business, it is characteristic for the manufacturer (one who is "integrated" and not just an assembler) to make the structure of the bike – the frame, fork, handlebars, wheels, and associated structural parts. Most of the "running gear" and accessories are purchased. In this case, it was imperative that there be strong supplier relationships with producers of tires, brakes, shifting systems, chains, saddles, pedals, grips, and several user changeable structural parts such as cranks and handlebar stems. In addition, supplier partnerships with providers of paint, labels, cartons, and steel were essential. Suppliers of additional parts such as hardware, printed material, supply items are always candidates for partnerships, but the crucial ones are those that provide major usage items. In this example, the suppliers of 13 components of the product were candidates for partnership. With multiple sourcing, and noncompeting providers of similar items, about 25 total suppliers make up the first tier of potential partners. I use the term *potential*, because not all commodity provider classes will have compatible or willing and able partners. In these, a more traditional buy-sell relationship will still prevail.

Where partnerships or alliances were to be developed, *the supplier must accept the responsibility to be cost and quality competitive (on a world class basis) if it is to hold up its share in the relationship.* Similarly the "integrator" (manufacturer) must also be competitive. When the various partners accept and realize these competitiveness responsibilities, the power of the total partnership is awesome. The old process of trying to trick or brutalize a supplier into a cost-competitive position can be replaced by the constant reminder of the responsibility it has taken along with the business. This also is a two-way street, which makes it fair for the supplier to admonish the customer who fails to maintain its competitive position. Better yet, each helps the other by sharing know-how to enhance their combined competitive position. The aggregate position of the suppliers and manufacturer can become one of a world class competitive enterprise, encompassing much of the value chain. Obviously, the distribution-retail partner is the missing link in a complete value chain – but that is another chapter's topic.

Where and How Does Partnering Start?

The successful partnership is best initiated near the top of the respective organizations. Someone at the V.P. level, at least, or, where possible, the president or CEO level is best suited to initiate the partnership. Some of the most successful partnerships in my experience began at the V.P. levels and then involved the top executive – this actually seemed to work better than purely "top down." The selection of which supplier(s) to begin with is also important. The first one(s) should be with a firm whose philosophy and strategy are most in line with the customer and where a strong buyer-seller relationship is already in place. This enhances and speeds the process. Success in the first few partnerships is also a real plus. It breeds enthusiasm and belief in the effectiveness of partnerships and bodes well for future attempts.

If the partners are in relatively similar stages of development and sophistication, this also enhances the process. When there are large differences in the stage of development of the two partners, an excessive burden is placed on the less developed side of the partnership. (Remember the Wal*Mart example previously cited.) The candidates chosen for partnership should be good-to-excellent suppliers at the outset. This not only increases the likelihood of success, but reduces the time and resources that must be devoted to developing the supplier. In virtually every case in my experience, some development (i.e., improvement) was needed by either the supplier partner or the customer partner to align their capabilities. As the importance of partnerships with suppliers became more evident, more customers became interested in developing them.

The initiator of the partnership was usually the more competent or more developed of the partners and undertook the job of bringing the other partner up to an acceptable competence level. This usually began with quality initiatives, then progressed to service and cost later in the process.

The first steps could take either of two directions. Beginning with sharing of strategic plans and directions is a good first step if the partners are both competent and well developed. I refer to this as *top down*. This provides both a basis for building trust in the relationship and assures congruence of strategic directions and goals.

If one partner is not very well developed, the best first step is a supplier survey and certification process. During the quality movement of the 1980s, many good forms of these were developed and documented. Whichever partner is more advanced in this respect should be the model for the partnership to use. This process ideally must start at a working level to proceed most rapidly. I refer to this as *bottom up*. In this way the stronger partner helps the weaker one develop at an accelerated rate. (An inherent assumption is that the weaker partner wants to improve rapidly and is willing to do "what it takes" to reach a level acceptable to the other partner.)

Once the approach has been selected (top down or bottom up), a move to sharing operating plans is in order. Instead of "throwing orders over the wall," this means a tighter linkage and sharing detailed production plans on a frequent (daily or weekly) basis. (The supplier scheduling previously described accomplishes this information sharing.) Downloading information directly from the customer's planning or scheduling system directly to the supplier creates a much closer linkage between the partners.

Partnerships As Easy Lead-in to Reengineering

The simple mechanics of how this is done can also eliminate the need for reams of paperwork or forms. This is an increasingly important concept as businesses reengineer their administrative processes to reduce non-value-added work. It is also one of the predecessors to invoiceless payment. There are several other rationales for payment without invoices, but all are based on "trust and partnership." In many cases, it is well known, understood, and documented (and physically inevitable) that certain kinds of purchased material had to be received and used in the course of making something to sell. (In bike manufacturing, we must have received a box if we were to pack a finished bike; in producing plastic desk accessories or chairmats, we must have received a given number of pounds of plastic resin if we produced a given number of plastic products). In these instances, why not just pay the supplier periodically, based on production records, and reconcile "shrinkage," waste, and so forth on a quarterly basis? Think of the simplification – no matching of receivers to purchase orders to invoices. Just extend the standard cost of the given material or component times the quantity produced, summarize once per day, week, month, or whatever, and cut a check (or better yet, transfer the money electronically).

All of the previous simplification (or reengineeering) is relevant provided the selection of who to partner with is done well and a solid, trusting partnership is formed. It virtually demands a consolidation from a large number of suppliers to a much smaller group. This has some inherent risk, so it must be undertaken with careful attention to which suppliers are in that smaller group and then communicating expectations, requirements, benefits, and so on. *Further, it is important to realize that no amount of development will turn a poor, unwilling partner into a good one.* This is why rigorous data gathering at the outset is important. Issues that are not exposed early can be devastating later. As soon as it is evident (usually by behavior, not words) that the supplier cannot or will not make the grade, steps should be taken to move away from a partnership involvement to one of buy-sell or elimination as a supplier altogether.

Partner Selection and Multilevel Partnerships

Screening suppliers for candidacy to become partners is a critical process. The checklist and assessment described earlier will make this process much less difficult. Also cited earlier, this important process cannot simply be delegated to a buyer or even the purchasing function alone. It needs to be a collaborative one involving the top level operating management of the company. In this way, all important factors (such as manufacturing operations' viewpoints, supply to competitors, financial strength, and systems competence) can be factored into the decision. Furthermore, all key areas of the company will have a vested interest in making the partnership work. The style, structure, strategy, and desires of the partners and their management teams must match. The culture of the parent corporations must be compatible. This is a more complex issue as "global" partners increasingly come not only from different companies, but from different countries. As the partnership progresses, more and more of the dealings will be directly between corresponding functional departments in the partner companies (and not through the purchasing-sales interface). Culture and language barriers and issues must be proactively addressed. Once this is done, the partnership can proceed to work on the "business" issues.

The partnership linkage on a multilevel organizational basis is the key to both supplier partnerships and customer partnerships, although the multilevel people-contact points change depending on which type of partnership it is. The previously mentioned multilevel partnerships spanning another level backward into the supply chain follow exactly the same process – involvement at different organizational levels – but starting high enough to assure solid support until trust is developed.

There must be top executive level partnering (at the V.P. and president or CEO level) to assure that the entire organizations of both partners understand the resources, support, and commitment that comes from that level. These should involve face-to-face meetings at least twice a year (more or less depending on the maturity and progress of the relationship). These should be "home and home" meetings. (Held at alternating sites of each partner.) Where the distance or cost of transportation is an obstacle, advanced telecommunications such as video-conferencing can help immensely. (Do not forget to schedule meetings with consideration for the partner's time zone and normal workday! Many a horror story has been told about the Japanese top executives who insisted on calling their American managers at 2:00 AM. In the United States, many Californians must rise before dawn to "attend" a tele-conference thoughtlessly scheduled by their counterpart on the East Coast at 9:00 AM.)

The meetings should have both private and "public" phases. In the private part, the top executives meet alone to discuss their perspective of how things are going and raise and resolve potentially sensitive or disruptive issues. This part of the meeting can be held before or after the more public part. It may be advisable to split it into two sessions, both before and after the main (public) partnership meeting. The open or "public" part of the meeting involves the functional team members from both partners and should revolve around a prescribed agenda of topics. Minutes from prior meetings (if it is not the first meeting), including agreed-upon actions, are distributed in advance and reviewed for progress, results, and obstacles (so that top management can collaborate to remove or resolve obstacles). New opportunities for improvement should be identified, perhaps brainstormed, and then moved to the "to do" list or put on hold for discussion at a future meeting.

Difficult issues or problems, such as failings in quality or service by the supplier, poor forecasting, inadequate lead times, or insufficient communication and information from the customer, are all fair game for this discussion. Refer to the "irritants" list for a more complete listing of potential problem causes. Someone at a fairly high level (V.P. of the host partner) should lead this meeting and keep it on track. It is ideal for a social event to precede the actual meeting (a dinner or reception), to allow personal acquaintances to be renewed up and down both organizations. The importance of this type event should not be minimized – it sets the stage for cooperative relations during the partnership meeting.

There are many other dimensions to this top management meeting. Some of these will be covered in the chapter on customer partnerships and others in the remaining chapters. Rather than try to cover too many nuances here, we should review the other kinds of partnership meetings that have proven effective. There are at least two others: the business (team) partner meeting and the functional partner meeting. These team meetings are essential to the customer partnership as well.

The business partner meeting consists of mid-to-lower-level working management in the functions that do the primary buying or selling and implementation of the agreed upon purchases and sales. This is the closest meeting to the old buy-sell relationship. The meeting and relationship at this level is really where the "heart and soul" of the partnership lives.

In the bike business at Huffy, we had a multifunctional, middle managers team that named themselves the Pro-TQ team (shorthand for procurement-total quality). People on this team were the drivers of the whole partnership process. That is why these meetings should occur frequently. They are usually held at the customer's location and should be directed primarily at meeting the ongoing needs of doing business with each other. All sorts of routine matters are handled here – forecasting, planning, general business condition adjustments, operating misunderstandings, error correction, problem identification (and resolution, if possible), new product introduction, quality or cost improvement progress, and so forth. More important, the momentum is sustained, and many issues are dealt with before they disrupt the partnership. Other working levels and parts of the two organizations actually do much of the work, but this level of teamwork is the "engine."

The Importance of Teamwork

Let me interrupt the line of thought for a moment to comment on teamwork – briefly! There are a lot of good examples of teamwork in business today, but teams and teamwork do not just happen. Many books, consultants, and excellent training and development organizations (like DDI) can provide help to build teamwork and teams [33]. *If your business does not already have a moderately good team environment and level of teamwork, stop reading this and go work on that.* You see, I have taken it for granted (up until now) that you know teamwork is essential, critical, imperative, mandatory (get the picture?) for success in any venture requiring cooperation among groups of people! With that caveat, let us return to the "how" of this partnering.

The *functional partner* meeting really maximizes the impact of teamwork in the partnership. This is not necessarily one meeting, but a set of meetings between the corresponding functional management (or cross-functional teams) of the two partners. This is where misunderstandings and problems that could grow from molehills to mountains in the old arms length relationship are brought to the surface, investigated, and resolved – and by the specific functional or team members closest to the facts of the matter. Participants who have responsibility for "planning" are ideal for these sessions. These meetings take a page from the principled negotiations concept of *Getting to Yes* [18].

An example of such a meeting might include (from the supplier's organization) sales, production planning, customer service, order fulfillment, and shipping-distribution-traffic personnel (and not necessarily the top level, the "working" level is the important one here) and (from the customer's organization) purchasing, forecasting-planning, order placement, receiving-distribution, and possibly freight or transportation people (from one or both). In the absence of a regular partnership meeting, this kind of meeting is usually triggered by some set of issues, problems or opportunities raised by one of the other two partner meetings (the top down one or the bottom up one).

Another type of functional partner meeting might arise around new product or process planning, development, or launch. This one might also be triggered by either partner. The customer partner might have a new product planned and wish to accelerate the development by the early involvement of the supplier. This is another trust building opportunity. Conversely, the supplier partner might be planning the acquisition of some new process equipment, technology, or capability that could provide improvements or advantages in the customer partner's product or material-component.

The Importance of Trust

Just as I did on teamwork, let me digress (again) for a moment on the topic of trust. It is probably worthy of its own chapter, but I will take the time to discuss it briefly now and then come back to it in each case to relate it to specific partnerships. Trust cannot be bought, cannot be mandated or dictated, nor can it be gained easily – but it can certainly be lost easily. It is something that builds up over a period of years yet can be torn down in a matter of hours. It has a lot to do with the people involved and how they behave, because the greatest of management philosophies and trust theories can dissolve quickly in the face of dishonest or untrustworthy people. Even a single person who is lacking in character and principle, who is in the first or second line of management contact with suppliers, can destroy trust between the organizations. Often, top managements "talk a good game" about trust and (think they) really mean it. Unfortunately, this message has to filter down through the organization (assuming they do really mean it). Unless this happens, the depth of conviction disappears, and the old adversary relationship creeps back in. Just review the lists of "irritants" and see how many relate in some way to mistrust. Trust can flourish only in the absence of doubt. (If I have doubts about your motives, about your integrity, or about your willingness or ability to follow through on a deal we made, I will not be able to trust you. Similarly, in the opposite case, you would not be able to trust me.)

An interesting perspective that reinforces the relationship and trust roles in partnership is very well stated by Pamela Coker, founder, president, and CEO of Acucobol, Inc. of San Diego [34]:

> Well, our relationships with our customers last longer than many marriages; for them, the relationship is an important business marriage. . . . If you regularly let your customers know that you "love" them, a high level of trust develops – a level of trust that is crucial for resolving technical problems. When you are "loved," you think more clearly, become more creative, and solve problems sooner.

What a refreshing outlook on relationships and trust!

Partnership Building Blocks and Trust

Until a supplier and customer have developed a relationship of trust, true partnership is very difficult if not impossible to achieve. The place to start with trust is simple – by telling the truth and being honest. First of all, it is simpler – you do not need a good memory because the truth will always be consistently the same. Second, it does not mean telling everybody everything, because it is often neither necessary nor in either's best interest to have certain information that should not be widely disseminated. However, when it comes to the firsthand working relationship, only honesty, openness, and truthfulness can lead to real partnership – and that is on both sides. The issue of trust could, as I have said before, fill the whole chapter or a book. Rather than dwell on it too long at this point, let us suffice to say that it is probably the most essential ingredient in building a real partnership. It is not only the most difficult to achieve and but the easiest to lose.

The next key building block to partnership could fall under several names: character, honesty, integrity, openness, communication. This point was driven home to me when I participated in a team-building activity that required us to do several things while blindfolded. If you want a little test to see how it feels when someone is not giving you the right amount or kind of information that you need, try this. Blindfold yourself securely in any environment and ask someone you know, even someone with whom you are fairly close, to just guide you as you go through some activities. You will discover just how much you take for granted about knowing the circumstances about your surrounding environment and how trusting you must be with someone whose behavior and guidance determines what your actions should be. Now imagine yourself as a supplier who is "blindfolded."

If you want an even more graphic test, blindfold yourself and put yourself in the control of three or more people as you listen to them talk about what should be done and find that they fail to communicate the situation to you very well, what the key decision issues are, and how they are going to help you make your decisions. You will quickly begin to understand what suppliers (and for that matter, in even more cases, your own employees or associates) feel like a lot of the time.

Another important point relates to the historical way of doing things. By sharing information openly, even if you are not certain or comfortable with it, a "vulnerability to change" is exhibited. The supplier scheduling was discussed earlier to illustrate that the important thing is to begin sharing the real plans – inaccuracies and all. What is important is to communicate with the supplier about your degree of confidence in a plan, a schedule, or a series of orders. In this way, the supplier can also "hedge" and will not be unpleasantly surprised if you find it necessary to make a change on short notice or of large magnitude.

The supplier partner may even have some good ideas how to reduce some of the risk of error. With today's technology, this is easier than ever – if only we decide (and start) to do it. In an *Industry Week* article entitled "Prosperity" [35] the path to sharing information to achieve partnership was described quite well: "The road to world-class supply-chain management meanders through a series of cultural changes – to a new plateau of trust. To achieve true partnership, customers and suppliers must share information – on new product designs, internal business plans, and long-term strategy – that once would have been closely guarded."

In fact, when really good communications are going on, a lot of the obstacles that add cost or lead time are exposed and removed, thus lowering the cost, improving the service, and building the relationship between the partners.

Partners Must Be Tough on Costs

Using this heading as a segue to the issue of how to negotiate cost in a partnership relationship, the answer is, "Not much differently than is done now but with a positive, win-win mind set rather than negative or win-lose mind set." It is even more important for a supplier to be cost competitive in a partnership role than in the old adversary role. This is true because the customer partner trusts the supplier partner to do so!

In many respects a customer is essentially an agent for the supplier. The customer is reselling the supplier's goods in some value-added form. If the supplier does not stay cost competitive, the net effect is that the agent or customer loses cost competitiveness and, thus, is in danger of losing business or failing totally. The difference in cost negotiation in a partnership environment is that it starts with a win-win mentality. McDonald's practices, cited earlier, are not always gentle. It knows how to throw its weight around with the best – so does Wal*Mart! Both have learned, sometimes from painful consequences, that it is usually better not to "wear the black hat." By partnering in the absence of threatening, people open up. Information is shared. There is a much deeper and broader involvement in what makes up the cost, where the opportunity areas are, and how to approach them for mutual benefit.

Whoever Provides the Greatest Value Wins

In this area the principles of team approaches to value analysis, value engineering, or backward supplier integration are extremely useful. The goal in any purchasing situation in a world class environment is to achieve the greatest customer value, which usually includes the lowest total cost. This is not necessarily the same as the lowest first cost. To achieve the lowest *total* cost, it is important that all of elements that add cost are clearly understood. The entire supply chain is involved, all the way back to the raw materials (suppliers) of your supplier through the handling, conversion, and delivery. All of these elements must be considered to see which parts of this entire chain do not add value. (Remember, value is defined by the customer.)

This concept of a multilevel partnership reaching back across two or even more supplier levels to achieve the desired closeness of linkage can be expanded further. Given the difficulty of forming just a single level partnership, too much time spent on discussing this advanced form would be inappropriate until the basic partnership is fully understood and in place.

Once again, unless there is a fairly high level of trust and honesty a supplier is often unwilling to expose its costs or supplier information to a customer for fear the customer will take unfair advantage of it. A supplier is usually willing, however, to discuss many of the elements that go into building up those costs. That discussion in itself is generally both revealing and productive. If a good job was done in selecting the suppliers, then those suppliers are good suppliers and they, too, are relatively cost competitive. They also have the right attitude about continuous improvement and maintaining their own cost competitive position. This is the best possible situation for a partnership. When these elements do not exist, the road to partnership is not impossible, just much longer and harder.

The whole concept of a partnership linkage is that a partner company maintains its cost competitive position on the purchased material it uses by selecting the best possible suppliers and depending on those suppliers to stay cost competitive in their own right. *It is very important that all partners remember the importance of adequate levels of profit and return on assets to the long-term viability of each other.* When this occurs, the price negotiation becomes much less an adversary and much more a partnerlike negotiation. However, do not be misled, there will be times when serious confrontation must occur. The key is to not let this confrontation turn negative (win-lose or lose-win), but rather to keep it on a win-win basis. If a win-win result cannot be achieved at that time, "no deal" (for the time being) is usually a better outcome than win-lose, which could taint future partnering efforts.

Identify Why and Write It Down

By recalling the economic needs of both organizations (usually to make and sell goods or services while earning an acceptable profit-return), the conversation can be redirected into a positive vein even if the confrontation cannot be resolved easily. One straightforward approach to focusing attention on the end results is shown in Figure 2.1, Statement of Partnership [36]. This can be done as a framed certificate signed by representatives at the vice president level of the supplier and customer companies and prominently displayed in their respective sales and purchasing departments. (Remember where the best place to start partnership discussions was?) Putting a statement in writing will not guarantee results, but it clearly states both partners' intentions. This can be very useful when

FIGURE 2.1

Statement of Partnership

The Smith company and Brown are initiating a new era in our business relationship: Partnering. Partnering transcends the traditional short-term relationship between customer and supplier in which each company focuses on its own goals with minimal concern for the other's business needs.

The new Partnering relationship is based on a shared strategic objective of satisfying the ultimate customer – the customer of Smith's products. The Partnering relationship includes visibility and support at Senior Management levels of Smith and Brown. Successful Partnering will lead to a sense of mutual interdependence. Brown will become a preferred supplier. Smith will become a preferred customer.

We recognize that our shared strategy requires continuous improvement in our total business relationship. Success on the journey of continuous improvement requires that we mutually:

- *Commit to innovative new growth ideas.*
- *Work together at the earliest possible stage of product development.*
- *Communicate effectively regarding our mutual goals and needs.*
- *Eliminate wasteful activity in our supply chain.*
- *Recognize the highest mutual quality standards as a way of life.*
- *Assure competitive cost of products to ultimate customers.*
- *Act in socially and environmentally responsible ways.*

We have identified a number of subjects for further study by Smith and Brown that will move us toward our shared strategic objective. Priorities will be assigned and working groups established to pursue these opportunities for mutual improvement. Benefits will be shared between Smith and Brown.

We pledge to work together to build trust and establish a long-term relationship characterized by candor and openness. We intend to continually improve our business relationship. We can always be better; we will never be as good as we can be.

John L. Mariotti
V.P. Purchasing / Operations
The Smith Company

Megan Zuckerman
V.P. Sales / Marketing
Brown Company

things seem to be getting off-track. It is also a good means for "cascading" the intentions of the partners throughout their respective organizations. The sample statement shown is a good one, but each partnership should tailor its own, specifically written to reflect its situation and goals.

A Legacy of Mistrust is Hard to Overcome

I hope that it is evident why I keep repeating the point that trust is one of the most important, perhaps the most important ingredient in a true, productive, and successful partnership. When so many years of mistrust have existed, trust is hard-won and easily lost. Both partners must know this and be constantly alert for opportunities to build trust and, even more important, on the lookout for places where trust can be damaged or destroyed. Sharing major new product or process information places a huge amount of trust that the other partner will keep the knowledge confidential and not misuse it to gain some economic advantage (even if not at the expense of the partner who confided the information). It is very tempting for even the most ethical sales organization to use "stories" about successes with other customers that could leak confidential information or be considered a breach of trust. This area is very delicate and bears constant watching.

Trust cannot be bought, it cannot be mandated or dictated, it can only be earned. It is somewhat transferable, but it is especially fragile during the transfer from one person to another. It builds slowly over time, but it can be lost in an instant. A level of trust that took years to build, can be destroyed in a matter of hours or days. Trust is very much about people – the ones who earn it, savor it, benefit from it, and appreciate it. When people in an organization change, as they inevitably do these days, the trust must be transferred and "revalidated," so to speak. Top management can believe in the trusting or trusted relationship and "talk a good game," but the commitment must permeate the organization from top to bottom. It must be a deeply ingrained part of the culture. Because of this, strong, genuine, lasting, and successful partnerships are very difficult to forge. In spite of this caution, partnerships are, I assure you, both possible and enormously powerful. Remember, nothing good comes easy.

Remember the Six Common Attributes

A partnership that will flourish is based on *honesty, integrity, fairness,* but also the understanding that *both partners must profit* from it – it *cannot be lopsided.* Neither is one partner responsible for the other's success or failure (although at times it must certainly seem that way). I mentioned Wal*Mart earlier, in the context of how powerful and demanding its people can be and how they can overwhelm a supplier to that firm's detriment. In fairness to the Wal*Mart people, in every case where I have dealt with them (and those are many), they have been extremely tough but fair. They let you know, up front, that they are going after the best value for Wal*Mart's consumers – and they do. If your company can provide it and compete effectively, you get the business. If you cannot, you probably will not. But, if there are extenuating circumstances that are not apparent, I have found them willing to listen and make adjustments, as in their Made in America program. They are also loyal to long-term suppliers, unless or until the supplier does not do its part by staying competitive and providing good service. I did not intend this to be a Wal*Mart "evaluation," but rather an illustration of one type of partnership (more on this topic in the next chapter). (It is easy to relate to Wal*Mart as a customer, because although it may not be "typical", its growth to over $75 billion in sales has made it the largest customer of many companies.)

Another temptation that size or power creates is to ask a partner for an unfair (or unearned) advantage at the expense of a competitor (who is also a customer of the supplier partner or vice-versa). The issue in this case is not whether the partnership will lead to a competitive advantage – given time to build, it will. It is tempting to try accelerating the advantage by asking the partner for unfair or unjustified preferential treatment (for example, charge you less or pay more) over a direct competitor.

While this may (or may not) be illegal under the Robinson-Patman Act, it may also be unethical (and unfair) unless there is a sound economic or business reason why the partnership yields a better deal that supports the preferential request. If a partner is asked or volunteers to provide a highly discriminatory deal, suspicion is warranted. Be very careful about asking for (or accepting) some discriminatory deal involving partners who deal with multiple competitors. In the words of one of my associates who helped me learn a lot about building supplier partnerships: "If they will do it for you, they will do it to you!" (And, as one associate always cautioned me, "large people don't look good in horizontal stripes!" It may be illegal!)

The last concept to touch on as we end this chapter is that *you are your supplier's agent.* You represent the supplier, its goods, and its services to your customers. If it has good products or services, that probably makes it easy for you to represent. If you do a good job on the value you add, everything can work out beautifully. If, however, you ask too much for its materials or services (or your own value added) or misrepresent the supplier in some way (intentionally or accidentally), you *harm both partners.* This concept of being an agent can help remind partners that a true partnership, like a marriage, is for "sickness and health, good times and bad." The only hope is that the "'til death do us part" does not describe the end of the partnership.

Up to this point all the approaches and concepts have been aimed at giving partnerships the best possible chance to succeed. They have been based on finding win-win solutions, participation, collaboration, cooperation, and so forth. There is a point when toughness must come into balance with participative, cooperative behavior. *Participation and partnership does not mean permissive or submissive behavior.* If you do not stand up for your rights, who will? If you don't hold firm when that is required, you will likely fail and take other partners with you. Only one thing is worse than a weak partnership: to be on the receiving end of a double-cross or victimized by an unethical "partner." In the old West, double-crossers got shot or hanged. Perhaps modern laws prohibit that extreme, but the message is clear.

Partnership is entirely consistent with tough but firm behavior. Ask anyone at Wal*Mart. Partners should not expect to be excused from the responsibilities they assumed when they entered the partnership. Conflicts must and will arise. To submerge them, avoid them, or ignore them only lets them fester and grow until they ultimately surface much larger, nastier, and harder to resolve. Bring up problems early and face them. Then resolve them – as partners.

One of my long-time "mentors" has been strategic planning "guru" Michael Kami. He is very emphatic about the importance of what he calls *Monday morning actions.* By this, he means: What are you going to do about this on Monday morning – different from what you are doing now?

To get this kind of thinking started right now, we finish this chapter with lists of the "top fives." By this I mean the top five partnerships that currently exist, the top five that you should start working on (Monday morning), and the top five that need some overhaul, rejuvenation, or termination. Write them here! *Then do something about them – on Monday morning.*

Monday Morning List

Best Five Supplier Partnerships:

1. _____

2. _____

3. _____

4. _____

5. _____

Five Partnerships to Start on (Monday morning):

1. _____

2. _____

3. _____

4. _____

5. _____

Five Partnerships in Need of Work (what kind?):

1. _____

2. _____

3. _____

4. _____

5. _____

Chapter 3

Partnerships
with Customers

KEY POINTS

- The purpose of a business is to create and keep a customer.
- Until a sale is made, nothing else good can happen.
- You do not make anything on the ones you do not sell.
- The customer is always right.
- When the customer appears to be wrong, reread previous statement.
- Do business the way the customer wants to do business.
- Face and resolve tough issues, don't ignore or finesse them.
- Information is power.
- The customer is either the end user or the link to the end user, and that is who defines value.
- Solid partnerships require the involvement of all levels and functions that work together at the respective partners.
- "We buy. You ship. You don't ship. We don't buy."

Of all the chapters, this is perhaps the easiest to write and the hardest to do. It should be easy to forge a partnership with a customer. The last quote on the list at the start of this chapter was spoken to me by a (now-retired) Wal*Mart merchandise manager, Bill Durflinger. Durf, as he was known, put it so simply, it's hard to miss the inference: The customer wants to be your partner, and both of you must understand what real partnerships are all about. They are a two-way street, with each partner responsible for his or her part of the deal. It seems so simple to bring about the change needed for things to work this way – but is it? This idea of change reminds me of the joke: How many psychiatrists does it take to change a light bulb? Only one, but the light bulb really has to want to change.

External Customers Pay the Bills

I will not confuse the semantics by discussing both internal and external customers in this chapter. Internal customers are really covered in-depth in the chapter on associate or employee partners. This chapter will focus on external customers – the ones that pay the bills. There are often two (or more) levels of external customers, so I would like to clarify that also before I go further. There is the ultimate "consumer or end-user" customer, and there is the "intermediate customer." An example of an intermediate customer would be a retailer, an installer, or a distributor of a product who purchases it from a manufacturer and resells it to an end user. Sometimes there could be several levels of intermediate customer (in the office products industry it is common). In any case, "pleasing the customer" means pleasing all of them. However, if you fail to please the next customer in the supply chain, you may never get a chance to please the end user.

Another way to think of it is what I have often called Mariotti's rule: You do not make anything on the ones you do not sell. Getting the order is still the tough part. Getting the second, third, and future orders is usually much more up to the "factory" than the sales department (based on how well the first order was serviced). In *The Marketing Imagination*, Theodore Levitt [4] says: "The purpose of a business is to create and keep a customer." What a wonderfully simple, yet powerful statement of why we are here (as suppliers).

After a customer has been "created" (or found, since in most cases they do already exist), keeping that customer is only part of the battle. The real goal is to keep customers and enjoy it – mutually – by making the relationship profitable and productive and last a long time. I have found no way of doing this that is more effective than becoming a true partner with the customer. After all, the intermediate customer is your "agent" with the ultimate consumer.

How well you, or your product does is often heavily dependent on how well your customer represents it and presents it. Much has been written about the lifetime value of a customer [37]. It is much easier and more profitable to grow volume with existing customers than to obtain new ones. Such growth far exceeds the value of newly won customers, because it costs far less to "keep one" than to "find" a new one. Because of this lifetime value, the partnership approach to customer relations is a good one, in that it provides both retention and growth potential.

Never, Ever Double-Cross Your Partner

The new paradigm of partnership is a two-edged sword – it cuts through the old paradigms, but it can do so painfully if one of the partners does not believe in or honor the doctrines of trust, open and honest communication, and mutual benefit. If either party tries to take advantage of the other partner, the entire relationship is at risk. Even if the unfair action goes unnoticed for some time, damage is done. The damage may be economic or, once discovered, psychological. Partnerships are a lot like marriages. They may not always last forever, but they are long-term commitments. They must be entered as if they must last forever, if the maximum benefit is to be gained from them. The HFD article [14] emphasizes this point: "In the euphoria over strategic partnering, the concept is sometimes misunderstood. Partnership can be an extremely overused word. . . . It's gotten to the point that if a vendor and buyer split a lunch tab, they call it a strategic partnership. True strategic partnerships, however, go way beyond the traditional relationships between buyer and seller."

The Value "Chain" Ends with the Consumer

Consider the entire value chain from raw material to end consumer. The previous chapter talked about the process of creating a partnership with the supplier side of the chain. This customer partnership (with the intermediate customer) provides the largest opportunity and yet the greatest risk to the supplier. The consumer is the ultimate customer that must be pleased and often is not the immediate customer. It is their definition of value that matters most.

Only the customer can provide solid information on the sales rate of a product. This allows the supplier to adjust capacity and supply to match the "real sales." These are the sales that provide service and timely delivery to end users, not just inventory for intermediate distribution. Distribution sales could be just "pipeline filling" (or depletion) and could mask the real success or failure of the product. They can cause damaging inventory buildup on one hand or poor service and lost sales on the other. The intermediate customer can provide access directly to the end user for feedback. This is another essential value of the strong partnership. Few products and their associated promotions or delivery are ideal when first launched. Adjustments can and must be made quickly to maximize the product's success (before some competitor discovers the needed adjustment and introduces a competitive product with the adjustment already made).

One example of waste (in the cost/value sense) might be in the kind of support materials like literature and packaging. Another might be in the distribution method of the product. This kind of waste is most easily avoided by close partnership with the customer. Often, a supplier packages the product for the "average case." This is usually exactly wrong. Some large customers will simply be forced to discard valuable packaging material to distribute and present the product the way they wish. Smaller customers will still balk at the absence of small case quantities and less display or presentation than they need (or too much if they do not use retail distribution at all). Literature that is suitable for the knowledgeable distributor is often far too technical or inappropriate for the consumer. Consumer assembly and use literature is too elementary and usually wasted on a distributor or its installer or technician. Tailoring the details of the product such as literature, packaging, distribution methods, merchandising (if it is a retail product), or protection from handling damage can all be done most effectively in close collaboration with the customer partner or consumer.

In this relationship with a customer, especially a very active one, there are numerous opportunities for "irritants" to arise. Jack Shewmaker's 1990 IMRA presentation itemized some of these irritants. I have expanded and generalized his list, and the revised list follows. The list vividly illustrates the diverse nature of irritants that can plague a partnership. While the list is still oriented to a retailer-supplier relationship, many of the items listed will sound familiar and be applicable to most customer-supplier relationships.

Key Irritants from the Supplier's Viewpoint:

- Confusing or complicated scheduling of appointments and meetings with buyers.

- Buying decisions attributed to anonymous sources such as "the committee" or simply "they."

- Execution of delivery, setup, installation, display, promotion different from what was agreed upon.

- Sudden changes in inventory needs – cutbacks or cancellations or unexpected surges in demand with little or no advance notice.

- Failure to keep planned meeting schedules or allowing meetings to be delayed inexplicably for hours.

- Sudden or major strategic direction or product specification changes.

- Last minute cancellation of promotions that had been organized at great expense and for which inventory has already been committed.

- Frequent buying staff changes or changes in the mix of assigned duties.

- Inaccessible senior management.

- Billing disputes and deductions.

Key Irritants from the Customer's Viewpoint:

- Stockouts, late delivery or poor quality.

- Backorders and long reorder cycles.

- Inadequate communications or poor information.

- Confusing or rapidly changing terms and allowances.

- Unrelated or unclear marketing campaigns.

- Frequent personnel changes in sales representatives or account managers.

- Incomplete or poorly thought out promotions or plans.

- Inadequate lead times on promotion plans.

- Inaccessibility to supplier management.

- Inexplicable policies (at least by the sales representatives).

- Billing disagreements.

- New product introductions or major product line changes with short or no advance notice.

- Decentralized and often autonomous multiple division structures where sales representatives from the same company sell closely related but different products to the same buyer, with differing terms, programs, and so forth.

Making the Most of the Partnership

When we reiterate the types of partner teams that should exist, it will become evident how this kind of "average solution," which does not deal with the ever-present "irritants," is damaging and wasteful and does not allow value maximization. A relationship that tailors product and presentation to the distribution system while overcoming irritants is only one of many ways a partnership can pay off. Sharing specific, timely, accurate consumer-end user feedback to the supplier is another. This book cannot possibly explore all the ways to benefit, because many of them emerge from the joint value-based analysis of the partner teams. I will attempt to use several different examples in illustration to raise the awareness of how many ways partnerships help build value in the business relationship. Not only can the product and presentation (packaging, merchandising) be altered as a result of this process, but entirely new products may be discovered, developed, and profitably exploited.

Take the examples of Newell and Rubbermaid in their many product categories. For those who aren't aware of Newell's breadth of product lines, they include Mirro, WearEver, and Anchor Hocking cookware; Levelor blinds; Bulldog and Amerock hardware; Intercraft picture frames; Goody hair care products; Sanford and Stuart Hall writing products; Lee Rowan storage; BernzOmatic torches; EZ Painter; and others. Rubbermaid sells most of its products under its corporate name with the exception of Little Tikes toys and Eldon desk accessories. Both companies have forged strong partnerships with key volume retailers, which have prohibited many competitors from gaining entry into their core markets. In these cases, a dominance of retail shelf space is created that in turn creates a dominant position in the mind of the consumer, as well as limits the selection from which consumers choose to that of the one dominant supplier.

The presence of partnership does not eliminate competition. However, if a strong continuing partnership is present, there is usually ample warning of competitive threats, and often an opportunity to respond "before the fact" (before the competitor gets in the door). The continuing honest communication in a trusting environment will expose competitive weaknesses in your product or program before you learn about them the painful way – by a competitor's presence and a loss of business.

If IBM and Intel had a stronger partnership, the handling of Intel's Pentium processor problems might have gone very differently. The two companies took widely differing positions on the likelihood of the error affecting the end user's planned use of the products. Both were in their own forms of "denial" (of each other and the facts of the situation). The result was damage to both – but especially to Intel. Intel failed to properly respond to its customers' concerns! This can only benefit competitors like Motorola, AMD, and others, both now and in the future. Contrast this with Johnson & Johnson's handling of problems with Tylenol, which respected customers' concerns and built good will.

But enough about how great it can be. How does it start, and what process keeps it growing and flourishing? The answers are a lot like the process described in the chapter on suppliers (the same relationship – one step further in the value chain). There is one big difference if both are viewed from the supplier who is "in the middle" of the value chain. With its suppliers, the purchaser can initiate the process, and the challenge is finding willing and able suppliers. In the case of customer partnerships, the competition for the sale makes the motivation in developing the partnership appear different. (It is not very different really, but perceptions are very important and the motive is often perceived as more self-interested in this case.) Others, if they are smart, are offering the same partnership possibility. Another competitor who has more to bring to the partnership, or is more sophisticated in the process, or simply has better relations at the top management level may win the preferred or favored partner role in a preemptive manner. J.C. Penney chairman W. R. Howell [13] comments: "Partnership concepts are changing the way retailers and suppliers conduct their business." This is why it is so important that this process be understood, initiated, and exploited – quickly! A supplier in an industry segment who perfects this ahead of others can erect formidable barriers to competitors.

Starting partnerships with customers requires that a relationship be established between fairly high-level executives of the two companies. This is easiest if it is based on a perceived need that one or both may recognize. Let us explore how each of these situations might work to create a partnership.

As was cited in the chapter on supplier partnerships, experience has proven that the V.P. level is an ideal place for a partnership to originate. Often the sales vice president of the supplier can originate the idea with the corresponding vice president of either purchasing or merchandise (selection) of the customer. The premise could vary – one of the best is the opportunity to grow faster and more profitably by partnering. Another is to blunt the thrust of a new or particularly troublesome competitor. This usually presumes that it will be at the expense of each other's competitors, but this is not always or necessarily the case. Partnerships are excellent ways for one of the partners to enter new segments or markets in a more efficient manner. New product introductions usually proceed faster and more effectively if a partnership relationship is driving them. (Adjustments also occur faster, leading to a higher success rate.)

A Pressing Need Is a Good Reason to Start

While growth in sales or profits is almost always the underlying reason for entering a partnership, there can be more immediate reasons. One partners may sense a competitive disadvantage that the other partner can help remedy. It may be that the supplier has a product the customer wishes to offer for sale or the customer has a presence with the end user or consumer the supplier wishes to have access to. The "competitive-disadvantage"-based partnership must be developed more carefully, because it is usually lopsided to the extent that one partner may benefit more than the other, at least initially. The current scramble for partnerships between telephone, cable, cellular phone, and computer companies is an excellent example of a "competitive-disadvantage"-based partnership. John Naisbitt's *Global Paradox* [38] discusses this situation in considerable detail. Because these dynamic-technology-based partnerships are often unbalanced, they may not hold up under competitive stress. However, any reason to initiate a partnership should be seized upon and nurtured, because the result a of successful partnership can be of immense benefit to both partners.

Once the vice president or someone at a similar (high) level has initiated the partnership concept, the working levels of both partners must be quickly brought into the dialogue. Bad feelings or problems (whether old or current, real or perceived) must be uncovered and worked through. This is a critical step if the partnership is to succeed. The working levels (buyers and sales people) must build strong relationships to make the partnership work properly. If they do not, issues that are "too small" to deserve higher management attention will be elevated in the partnership meetings and can have a chilling effect on the relationship and the progress. Assuming the people at the working level have either good or excellent relations already, the partnership has a head start.

Top Management Commitment

The next step is to gain commitment from the top of both partners' organizations. The top means the highest ranking executive that can reasonably be responsible for the business unit, division, or corporation that is the parent of the partners. If one or both partners represent divisions, at least the division general manager must be so committed. If the partner is a solely or privately owned entity, the principal owner and the CEO (if it is not the same person) should be committed to the partnership. To clarify one point, it is difficult for someone to become committed to something he or she does not understand. It is critical that the concept of partnership be understood fully by the top management of both partners. A tempting trap is to paint the partnership in a favorable light for the top executive, glossing over how tough issues will be dealt with. *Do not do this!* There are few times that I am willing to say "do this" or "do not do this." This is one of those times.

A partnership represents a strong commitment by both partners. It is designed to help each succeed more effectively than an arms length relationships would. It will not be without problems and issues. The relationship does provide a better platform for airing and resolving tough issues and disputes, but it is not a panacea. Top management must understand this. The partnership is for good times and bad. It will help in both – but only if both partners realize that part of sharing the gain may be temporarily sharing the pain (in a tough market, for example). As stated at the conclusion of the prior chapter, this does not mean partnership in the old subservient, misdirected sense (you give and I take). Firm, fair, win-win deals are sound bases for today's partnerships.

Everybody Has to Buy In

There may be intermediate levels of organization between the buyer-seller and the vice president. These people (remember all organizational "levels" and "functions" are staffed by people who must "buy in" to the partnership) need to become involved. This is best done by those at the buyer-seller level presenting the concept of the partnership to gain others' commitment. Often this will occur as the attempt to get the vice president involved occurs. Sometimes it occurs "top down" when the vice president is the initiator of the partnership, but somehow it must occur. Similarly, where functions outside the buying and selling roles are heavily involved in supplier-customer selection, presentation, servicing, and operating relations, those people must become involved and "buy in." Areas such as logistics, order fulfillment, and new product development offer huge opportunities for partnering success.

From Boundaryless to Bandwagon

If this sounds like a far-reaching, extensive process, it is! A truly successful partnership extends top to bottom and side to side across both organizations. There is, to a great degree, a "boundaryless" feeling to it. While the legal entities may have boundaries as companies, the working relationship, in its ideal state, almost ignores those boundaries. This requires a great deal of ethics, integrity, and maturity in the people of the two partners. The ideal state is to be strived for, although it is only seldom achieved. Even if this ideal linkage is not fully achieved, the partnership can be very effective. A sort of "bandwagon" effect occurs as the relationship builds. Behaving like a true partner with this supplier (or customer) becomes "the thing to do." Once the first pass at establishing relationships and uncovering opportunities, issues, problems, and so on has occurred, a process can begin.

Those at the working levels, up to and including the V.P. level, must meet periodically to keep things on track. If the top management can be present for part of this meeting or a social gathering preceding it (a very good idea) to show their support and sponsorship, all the better. Those at the direct working levels already meet regularly (or at least they should). This connection should be expanded horizontally in both organizations to involve support functions. Since people in these functions often do not travel to the other's site, such excursions should be planned. Because of cost and time, after a partnership gets going, these site visits can be less frequent. In the early stages they should be more frequent, because they are invaluable in building awareness, appreciation, and comfort with the partner's situation and people. After the partnership begins building momentum, the "home and home" visits can be situational (to work on a specific problem or opportunity – a delivery problem, perhaps, or a new product, process, or system introduction).

As in the supplier partnership, we have now outlined the people contacts needed. These are the hardest to develop. Once these have begun developing, the partners can agree on what kind of systemic interaction they will have. How will information be shared? Who is responsible for doing what, by when, and how?

People Partner First, Companies Partner to Last

It is necessary to digress a moment here. Partnerships are between people first and companies second – even though we may talk as if it were the inverse. For the partnership to last as people change jobs, companies, and roles, it is necessary for the partnership to evolve to a relationship between the "companies." But, make no mistake, it starts (or ends) between and with people. Whenever people come together to achieve something, a few basic rules must be followed or the meeting and its results may turn out poorly and "poison" the partnership unnecessarily. A recent article in the Apparel Merchandising section of *Discount Store News*, "Cyber Trust: Will It Work?" [39], opens with these words:

> Trust is an essential element of any successful marriage. Partners, committed for life, often share details of their personal and psychological selves with their mates; it's an expected and essential form of mutual support. Now apparel retailers and manufacturers are reciting their vows, and forming close give-and-take relationships that wed their businesses together in unprecedented ways. Linked together through cyber space with electronic management tools, both partners are sharing proprietary sales information, consumer research and future marketing plans and promotions. The concept of category management, a complete system of product administration that marries supplier and store, may permanently change the relationship between buyer and seller.

Adversarial relationships, once a common dynamic in retailing and manufacturing communities, have no place in category management, whose proponents describe it as something akin to a match made in mercantile heaven. "It really is a partnership, not just some kind of lip service."

Systems and Processes Matter, Too

Discussing strategic partnerships in HFD, Chuck Rosner of Ekco says, "The relationship between companies is going to be shaped by the systems of strategic partnership, such as EDI, quick response and ECR (Efficient Consumer Response) ...." I am not sure I would go quite that far, but without a doubt, the systems and the shape of the relationships will be inextricably intertwined to create a truly singular, effective purpose – serving the end user-consumer. To achieve such a lofty goal, sound management principles must be used throughout the partnership process.

There should be a published agenda for all partner meetings, at least a list of topics and time frames, distributed in advance (by the host or whoever instigated the meeting) so all parties can prepare. Poor preparation will cause an unproductive meeting, and this too can taint the partnership. Some topics will be difficult to resolve in a large meeting and may be better assigned to a smaller group to work through. Make sure the group is composed of people with sufficient authority to resolve the issues – do not delegate problems down the organization to bury them. Doing this will surely doom the partnership.

Finally, it is imperative that someone keep good minutes, the essence of which should be written on an easel at the front of the room, visible to all. The common visibility helps minimize cop outs later and provides confirmation of agreed-upon actions, plans, assignments, and so forth. As the pages of the easel are filled, they should be displayed around the room for continuity. All subjects should be brought to some resolution, even if that is to table them until another meeting. Unresolved issues can be shown on a "parking lot" page of the easel pad. Often these will resolve themselves during the meeting. If they do not, they can be addressed near the end of the meeting or go on the minutes as unresolved issues. (Try to keep these to a minimum, because they are a form of procrastination, but do not let one sticky issue derail the meeting either.)

What Gets Measured Gets Done

The final topic in meeting protocol is that the minutes should take a format that provides a checklist for action: What was the topic? What action or direction was agreed upon? Who takes responsibility for resolving or acting on it? (Do not list function or department names, list people's names wherever possible.) When will the action or resolution be complete? (If a supplementary schedule is required, call for it as the deliverable, along with end dates.)

A good format for the minutes includes a formalized outline of *who* will do *what* by *when* and may include *why, how,* and *who* will follow up or report on the progress (minutes should not be a narrative). It is important to be very specific about who is responsible, otherwise vague assignments will float aimlessly around, being done by no one. Timing should be reasonably aggressive, and a follow-up system should trigger a check to see if "it" was done as planned and agreed.

After a series of these follow-ups (preferably by one of the highest executives present), the message will start to get around: "Take these partnership agreements, assignments, and deadlines seriously – they are important!" As stated earlier, it may help to write down the goals and conditions of the partnership. A typical statement of partnership agreement is shown in Figure 2.1. Such a document reinforces the reasons and importance of the partnering it describes. The intentions of those signing it and living within its words will really determine the effectiveness of the partnership.

Once the partners' meeting has been completed, this format of minutes provides both a means of sharing the outcome with other people, who need not be involved in the meeting or only attended part of it, and a means of reporting on the progress or follow-up action required. The minutes are also a way of raising awkward issues for future group attention. Any misunderstanding about who will do what by when can be easily flagged before a misunderstanding is created or elevated to a dispute (where positions could become entrenched or polarized for the sake of personal pride or risk of embarrassment). This minutes format provides the start of the agenda for the next meeting. Since one of the most troublesome things in business is to schedule meetings that involve numerous busy people, the next meeting date(s) should be chosen and agreed upon before this meeting breaks up and then be confirmed in the minutes.

Partnering Is So Obvious, Why Not Do It?

A common reaction to the topic of partnerships is that it is so obvious, of course, everyone should do it. Wrong! Many people need to develop their own principles, practices, processes, and so forth before they can be much of a partner. Many others do not do it because they just cannot quite take the first step. Others get started and the first obstacle derails the partnership because either the commitment was not there or no one was able or willing to deal with obstacles and conflict. You see, many of the partnerships that fail do not fail for good reasons. They fail because of poor management, weak leadership, misunderstandings, assumptions about others intentions, incorrect perceptions, and other interpersonal reasons. Most of all, they fail because of mistrust. By using well-defined processes, many of these can be avoided or minimized and dealt with while they are still small and manageable. Trust is not built in one large leap; it is the result of many small events – commitments made and kept.

McDonald's was described earlier as a pioneer of partnerships. This grew it out of necessity. McDonald's was blazing new trails, and no one in the existing supplier ranks knew how to service them as it did so. In many respects, the people at Wal*Mart were in the same boat. What they were doing looked deceptively like what other discounters did, but it was not. That was how Wal*Mart could grow and dominate the mass retail industry over the short span of about two decades. For a large part of my career I have worked with Wal*Mart as it grew into a retailing giant. During the first part of that era, Jack Shewmaker was the vice chairman and the top operating person with whom I dealt. Jack has believed in partnerships for a long time, and his words spoken back in 1990, reprinted recently in *Inside Retailing* [40], ring loud and clear today as surely as they did then. These words say it so well, I will quote them in their entirety here. His "action plans" are shown in Figure 3.1.

Identify from 20–50 of your suppliers. Accumulate and collect all the data you can on these suppliers; then decide upon a partnership approach and spread this word throughout your organization by continuous buyer-group meetings.

Then expand buyer meetings into meetings with all of the support functions personnel.

In the process of doing this, recognize that we, through delegation, over, and adversarial encouragement have created "power zones," wherein individual buyers or departments have been given authority, which precludes partnership relations. Convert them to modern management techniques.

Above all, don't forget that in today's age of information technology, many support functions are already in the mainstream of the buying and selling of merchandise. Transportation, distribution, data processing, accounting and store operations are integral to the buying function in today's high-tech environment.

With this being the case, many of us must redefine the buyer's role ... because it must change.

Now, while you are in the process of collecting data on your suppliers, identify all known problems that apply to each. Then contact senior personnel of the suppliers along with their salesmen and their sales team. Request an audience, assign your own support team, then schedule meetings between the two groups.

At these meetings discuss known problems but be sure to devote equal time to discussing mutual opportunities and long-range planning objectives. Take an actionable point of view where individuals on both teams are assigned responsibility with deadlines and goals. At the senior management level maintain responsibility for follow-up.

FIGURE 3.1
Jack Shewmaker's Partnership Steps

Supplier Approach

1. Identify key retail accounts.
2. Develop internal plan.
3. Redefine salesman's role.
4. Assign key team members.
5. Seek an audience with retail counterparts.
6. Do homework on Industry and Technology.
7. Be prepared to solve problems.
8. Offer new ideas.
9. Do long range planning.
10. Commit plans to writing.
11. Set goals and follow up.
12. Maintain multilevel contact.

Retailer Approach

1. Identify 20–50 suppliers.
2. Collect data on all suppliers.
3. Conduct internal buyer group meetings.
4. Address power zones.
5. Involve support functions.
6. Redefine buyer's role.
7. Identify all problems.
8. Contact supplier senior personnel.
9. Assign support team.
10. Schedule meetings.
11. Discuss problems and opportunities.
12. Do long range planning.
13. Assign responsibilities.
14. Follow up and review.

Source: A sign in the foyer of the headquarters of Manco Inc.

This advice coincides almost exactly with my own views – whether looking at the relationship from the manufacturer's or from the retailer's viewpoint.

A simple story illustrates how partnership can succeed or fail over small misunderstandings. One day a man was walking down the street. He saw a parked truck and a man nearby struggling with a very large, heavy bundle against the truck – part of it on the truck and part off. The passerby, feeling generous, offered to help. The worker, tired of wrestling with the heavy bundle gladly accepted his help. The two men situated themselves on opposite sides of the bundle and, for the next several minutes, struggled mightily with it. After what seemed like an eternity, but was really only a couple of minutes, both stopped struggling with the bundle. They backed away from it and, sweating profusely, spoke between gasps. The worker spoke first. "I never thought it would be so hard to get this bundle off the truck," he gasped. The passerby's response was "Off the truck? I thought we were trying to put it on the truck!" What a large difference a small misunderstanding had made. A little communication at the start of the job would have made a world of difference in their success or failure. To end the story, with the purpose clearly understood, they easily hefted the bundle off the truck onto the street. Had they given up without persistence, communication, and a mutual need to achieve their goal and understand each other, all their efforts would have yielded nothing but wasted energy.

Good Things Do Not Come Easy

So often it happens this way with partnership attempts. Few good things come easy, and nearly all require following a defined process to achieve success. Figure 3.1 outlines the process in its simplest form. Once the process has begun, follow-up, using the checklist and development list in Figures 3.2 and 3.3, becomes a very important factor in keeping the progress moving and identifying and removing obstacles. One common obstacle is a single influential person who is skeptical, cynical, or just not committed to the success of the partnership. If the partnership is truly important, management must be ready to deal with this kind of an obstacle (even through reassignment or termination of the person, if necessary). I hope the next chapter will provide some added insights in how to build partnerships among associates-employees and eliminate many of these types of obstacles.

FIGURE 3.2

Checklist for Customer Partnership Effectivness

___ 1. Build/enhance functional relationships

___ 2. Exchange information freely

___ 3. Ensure complete product representations

___ 4. Accelerate moving product to market

___ 5. Increase the awareness/use of related corporate units

___ 6. Increase productivity of inventories

___ 7. Increase effectiveness of organizations

___ 8. Improve profitability

___ 9. Reduce poor selling/obsolescence/ unprofitable incidents

___10. Improve relative competitive position

___11. Build dominant competitive advantage

Source: "Gaining Competitive and Commercial Advantage: Developing Strategic Partnerships." Coopers & Lybrand proposal for consulting services.

FIGURE 3.3
Process for Partnership Development

- Initiate the process of building relationships with people

- Understand the current state of both businesses, honestly and realistically identifying key success factors, market situation, and so forth

- Develop strategic profiles – check for mismatch or fit of strategies, including marketing, distribution, operations, information

- Conduct a detailed business assessment – sales, profitability, inventory performance, and so on

- Develop a strategic program to use the information jointly developed to improve the strategic and tactical plans

- Define performance measurement and objectives and agree on them

- Communicate the agreed upon plans to all personnel necessary to implement them (many should have been involved in the development)

- Begin implementation, checking progress frequently at first, resolving issues that arise, making adjustments

- Follow up continuously, again and again until progress is evident (if it is not, reconvene the group to diagnose the obstacles that are impeding progress – use the assessment to help)

Now it is time to again make the "Monday morning action" lists. List the five best partners and think about why those partnerships work. Then list the five that do not work and try the partnership assessment worksheet on them. It is not always easier to fix a broken partnership than to start a new one, but often it is. It is almost certainly faster. Last, list the five partnerships that you know you should form and decide what you will do on Monday morning to get moving on those. Write it down here.

<u>Monday Morning List</u>

Five Best Customer Partnerships:

1. _____
2. _____
3. _____
4. _____
5. _____

Five Most in Need of "Fixing":

1. _____
2. _____
3. _____
4. _____
5. _____

Five That Should Be Started Now:

1. _____
2. _____
3. _____
4. _____
5. _____

Chapter 4

Partnerships with Associates and Employees

KEY POINTS

- "No man can build a business. A man builds an organiztion, the organization builds the business. It can be done no other way."
- Ordinary people can do extraordinary things.
- "Associates" are more effective than "employees."
- A fair deal is one you would take either side of.
- Be consistent and present both expectations and limitations.
- "If you don't trust your associates to know what is going on, they know you don't really consider them partners."
- Beware of filtered information, but don't kill the messenger.
- Small group meetings are effective, but listen to everybody.
- Constantly restate the "vision" – be a "Johnny one-note."
- Training is the only investment on which the return can be infinite.
- The employer generally gets the employees he or she deserves.
- Do unto others as you would have them do unto you.

I have had about 30 years of experience dealing with "employees," "associates," and "partners." In the process of writing about what I learned from these relationships, I began looking for corroboration of my beliefs. It was not hard to find. Then I began looking for conflicting views that might undermine my convictions. I found very little. A lot of people have gotten ahead in the world by being users or manipulators, but I think their victories are temporary. Sooner or later "they'll get theirs." The old saying about what comes around goes around is true in this context, too.

In April 1983, I had the terrible task of telling all of my associates at the Oklahoma Bicycle Division of Huffy that our plant and division were closing – through no fault of theirs. The company simply had too much bike capacity for the depressed market; and the Celina, Ohio, plant was the biggest and most mature, so it would be the survivor of the three (the smaller California division had been shuttered in 1982 and its production moved to Oklahoma). I had seen the day coming for several months and dreaded it.

I had agreed to accept the position of president of the sole remaining division several months earlier, but this could not be disclosed until after the Oklahoma closing had been formally voted on by the board and announced to the public. The morning consisted of four meetings: one with my direct staff, who pretty much knew what was happening; one with the remainder of the salaried work force; one with the "city fathers," who had been so supportive and cooperative over Huffy's 3 years there; and finally one with the 500 hourly employees. These 500 were the "survivors" of a vigorous weeding out process; and they were good, loyal, productive people. Nothing they could have done would have kept the plant open. The first meeting was not so bad, because my staff had been prepared. I got a little emotional, but kept it mostly under control. The second meeting was a lot harder. The salaried group and I had been through a lot together. I broke down in tears, briefly. Then, after a couple of deep breaths, I answered questions for 30 minutes. The city leaders were next. These included some personal friends and people who had "gone the distance" to get us training help, tax abatement, a new road, and so on. It was a rerun of the salaried group meeting: some tears, some desperate pleas to see if they could help in any way to keep the plant open. The city would be losing its second largest employer. Finally, it was over.

Then came the really tough one – with the hourly workers. By this time, I knew the informal grapevine from the salaried group meeting must have leaked word of the news to the plant, which was connected to the offices. I was surprised when I received a polite round of applause as I stepped to the podium. In spite of a lot of deep breaths and much resolve, I could not contain my emotions. I still get choked up writing about it. These people had come from far and near, from farms and villages, a few even from the oil fields. They had survived all the start-up troubles, from machine malfunctions to broken plumbing. They had struggled to learn how to build bikes with a speed and precision that would measure up in a company widely regarded as the most productive bike producer in the world. And they had done it! Quality was even better than in the mature Ohio plant, and productivity was closing in on that plant's levels. Customers loved to buy the bikes produced there – they simply worked right and all the parts were there, too!

Now, because of some macro-economic reasons that I was going to try to explain, they would be out of jobs soon.

As I stood at the mike with tears streaming down my face, they waited patiently for me to tell them what they already knew was going to happen to them and why. Finally, I was able to get the words out. When I finished and prepared to leave the podium, I received another round of applause – this time not just polite but hearty. I was floored. Over the 3 months that ensued, I found that they had truly responded to my appeal to "go out in style." Quality improved. Productivity stayed high. Part of it was, no doubt, due to the fine vice president of operations, John Simonis (now deceased), who designed the plant, opened it, operated it through start-up woes, had it humming, and had to shut it down. I am sure he shed his own tears, perhaps less visibly because of his stoic persona, but nonetheless he hurt in his own way.

What does this story have to do with partnerships? It embodies the very essence of partnerships. We pulled together as partners. We were successful as partners. And, when the time came to shut down, we all shared the pain, the grief, and the pride as partners. I left Ponca City, Oklahoma, about 11 years ago. That fateful day was April 13, 1983 – a day after my birthday. As I reflect back, I consider it to be an awful birthday that year, except for one thing – the support of the partnership with the people of that plant. Their applause remains the saddest and happiest memory of my business career. With this philosophical preamble, let us get on with the meat of this chapter.

As an appropriate segue from the topic of customer partnerships to that of employee partnerships consider the statement of Fred Reichheld of Bain & Associates [41]: "It's impossible to build a loyal book of customers without a loyal employee base. It's like trying to build a brick wall without mortar." In his most recent book, *The Age of Paradox* [42], English author Charles Handy offers a

simple explanation for how the turmoil in corporate organizations has come about.

- No longer do people believe that those at the top
  necessarily know best.
- No longer can the leaders do all the thinking for the
  rest.
- No longer do people want them to.

Pretty sobering thoughts, considering the way most
people in businesses have behaved for decades. There
seems to be a spreading awareness that the executive
suite has no monopoly on "brain power."

The Research Confirms What We Suspect

Reflecting on these three rather simple but significant
statements, I began searching for confirmation or at least
clarification. I came across a superb research report coau-
thored by Rich Wellins of DDI and Ann Howard of the
Leadership Research Institute [32]. Not only is it compre-
hensive in scope, but it is current, resulting from a recent
follow-up to a survey done several years ago. The introduc-
tory two paragraphs hit home so well, I will not even
attempt to paraphrase from them. Here they are:

Leaders Are Performing on a New Stage

Organizations are changing – they must to compete in today's demanding economy. Many
approaches to change, such as total quality management, reengineering, and self-managed teams,
depend on employee involvement and empowerment. Such practices allow organizations to tap
into the creativity and energy of their employees to
an extent that is not possible with traditional
forms of management. High involvement not only

promises a way to tackle today's problems, but builds flexibility to respond to tomorrow's challenges.

Although high involvement can help enhance organizational competitiveness, it is not a simple solution. Associates cannot be empowered in a vacuum. They cannot be expected to assume new functional responsibilities and authority without a great deal of guidance and support from their leaders. This means that the roles of the leader must change dramatically.

I will cite more findings of this study as we move through this chapter. Now let us consider further how roles change as partnerships become the goal.

A Rose by Any Other Name ...

The title of this chapter alone signals a change in the name of who we are talking about. Some of the most successful and respected leaders in business today have already proven that the name we call our "employees" does make a difference – if we truly live it in our behavior. At Wal*Mart, Sam Walton made it clear that they were not "employees," they were "associates." And he meant it and lived it. In his autobiography [43], he devoted an entire chapter to "Building the Partnership." The opening lines of that chapter are so well stated that they deserve repeating here:

As much as we love to talk about all the elements that have gone into Wal-Mart's success – merchandising, distribution, technology, market saturation, real estate strategy – the truth is that none of that is the real secret to our unbelievable prosperity. What carried this company so far so fast is the relationship that we as managers have been able to enjoy with our associates. By "associates" we mean those employees out in the stores and in the distribution centers and on the trucks who generally earn an hourly wage for all their hard work. Our relationship with the associates is a partnership in the truest sense. It's the only reason our company has been able to consistently outperform the competition – and even our own expectations.

I had the privilege of knowing "Mr. Sam," not nearly as well as I would have liked but well enough. I can recall a day in the mid-1980s, one that I will never forget. I was president of Huffy Bicycles, and we were fighting an attack on our U.S. market by the Taiwanese and Korean producers. We held our market share, thanks in a large part to Wal*Mart's Buy American program. I was invited to attend a store managers' meeting where about 4,000 Wal*Mart managers and associate and assistant store managers gathered. I sat on the stage with about ten other "Made in America" suppliers. Each of us made brief remarks to the assembled group. The room was draped with huge charts showing Wal*Mart's growth in sales and profits. The theme of the meeting was "Yes, We Can!" (make the objectives for the next year).

I will never forget Mr. Sam speaking to that group, describing changes Wal*Mart was making in the policies for associates in simple English, with his own special flair. When he finished, David Glass, his appointed successor, joined him at the microphone. David is much more soft-spoken than Sam, and he simply walked up to the mike and, with his arm around Sam's shoulder, quietly asked if the managers thought "we could make our goals for next year." As if they were connected (because, you see, they were – emotionally), 4,000 people leaped spontaneously to their feet, thrust their fists skyward and yelled, "Yes, we can." My thoughts then, as now, were, "how can anyone beat this kind of emotion and unanimity of purpose?" And no one has.

Less dramatic, but just as important, a story is related by Stanley Gault, former CEO of Rubbermaid and now CEO of Goodyear. He tells about encounters with truck drivers, and stock workers in Rubbermaid's huge Wooster, Ohio, plant. His description emphasizes how they could accept and relate to him as their "associate," each with different jobs to do, rather than as their "boss." Gault was gone from Rubbermaid before I got there, so I missed the experience of actually working with him. It is clear from his success there and at Goodyear, that he, too, does not just call employees associates, he means it.

With those two stories as the preamble, let us reflect on the situation closer to home – your own business and personal associates.

If You Want Only One Rule: The Golden Rule

Through most of the course of your life you will probably be someone's employee. If you are successful, you will attain the responsibility of supervising other employees and certainly have relationships with numerous peers who hold positions similar to yours. The nice part about this chapter is that one rule could fairly well sum it up. But then there would not be much to the chapter, if I did not expand on that rule – so here it is anyway. The Golden Rule applies: *Do unto others as you would have them do unto you.* I know it sounds "corny," but it is important – very important. It is almost hard to figure out where to start describing why and how it is so important. Let us start with the situation where you are "the boss." You have a partnership with your employees.

You expect something of them and they expect something of you. The first step is to make sure that you both fully understand what those expectations are. Frequently this step is skipped over, and it lies at the bottom of all the problems that follow after it. The step requires solid two-way communication. I said two way, which means listening, not just talking. That is the second most violated rule. Too many "bosses" think being a good communicator means simply telling people what to do and not listening to the valuable feedback as to why that may or may not be possible, difficult, practical, and so on. Next, be sure that all share a good understanding about the limits of what you can do for them (ideally, not to them). If you lack the authority to get resources for them or to make decisions, be sure that is understood up front, as well as the fact that if you believe in their position or what they need, you will go to the higher authority and seek that support. Much of the frustration felt by employees everywhere originates because someone in a leadership position failed to communicate fully or well (or honestly?).

Honesty Is Everything

We talked about two-way communication and understandings, next we will talk about honesty and openness. You need not tell the employees everything; sometimes it is not in their best interest or yours for them to know everything (some bad news may simply demoralize them, raise unfounded concerns, and serve no constructive purpose). Truthfulness, however, is tremendously important. If you cannot or should not tell them something, tell them honestly that you cannot or should not tell them so; it has nothing to do with your respect for them, but rather with the circumstances surrounding that information. They will still want to know and may still not be satisfied without being told, but at least they will respect you for what you have told them.

On the subject of respect we can hardly mention the word without getting into the word *trust*. In "Managing with a Conscience" [44], Frank Sonnenberg says it pretty well: "Without trust, marriages fail, voters become apathetic, and organizations founder. Without trust, no company can ever hope for excellence." A key finding of the Development Dimensions International (DDI) study [33] was that "Senior/higher managers significantly underestimated the extent to which frontline employees' motives, *especially their distrust of management,* pose significant barriers to high involvement. Leading the list was the perception that frontline employees don't trust management" [my emphasis added].

It is important in your partnerships with employees and associates that you be trustworthy. If you tell someone you will do something, do it. If you cannot or do not intend to do it, then do not tell the person you will. Be consistent as much as possible. Almost nothing is harder to deal with than an inconsistent boss. One day up, the other day down – and never sure which is which until there is trouble. Consistently high expectations are much better than widely variable ones (provided those expectations are clearly communicated and employees receive honest and truthful feedback as to how they are doing in their pursuit of the objectives outlined). When the respondents in DDI's survey were asked to evaluate the importance of leadership roles, the most important role behavior was modeling trust, described as "be consistent in words and actions." One of the respondents, at the associate level, stated it very clearly, "Consistent behavior should be a constant of someone in a leadership role. If this doesn't exist, the trust breaks down and the whole ship begins to sink."

In these days of employee involvement and empowerment, one of the most common errors is a failure to specify the limits, so those employees who are being involved or empowered do not become frustrated or demoralized by coming up against such limits only after they have developed a plan (worse yet, when they have developed a successful plan and find out too late that they did something unacceptable in getting there because of not knowing their limitations in advance). One associate discussed the problem of leaders "letting go." "There is still quite a lot of telling us we can do something and then not allowing it (for example, to shut down a line because of too many problems and when we go to do it, it isn't allowed)." Another associate went so far as to put such thoughts into words, "A person has to 'want' to be empowered to make it work." A third put it differently, "When we get really busy, everyone reverts to old habits (don't bother me with philosophy, I have too much work to do)" [33]. Is it any wonder partnerships with associates are more easily talked about than done? It takes hard work to make it really work!

Feedback Tells Us How It Is Going

On the subject of feedback, many companies have formal performance appraisal systems but few companies have effective ones. Imagine yourself out for a night of bowling with one difference; you throw the ball, you hear the sound of it hitting the pins but you never get to see how many pins you hit nor do you have any idea where those remaining stand on the alley. At the end of the evening, no score is recorded. How satisfying an evening do you suppose it would be? People need feedback. They need to know how they are doing. They especially need to know how they are doing if they are doing poorly. In most cases someone who is doing poorly realizes it or suspects it and agonizes over it far more than most managers or bosses realize.

I am reminded of the story of a local Chamber of Commerce meeting where the speaker was addressing the crowd about the importance of feedback. He asked if anyone wanted to volunteer a definition of feedback. The chicken farmer raised his hand and was recognized. He rose to speak. "About 6 AM everyday I get up and feed my chickens. From 9 'til 11 they give me feedback!" After the laughter subsided, the crowd realized that some (bad) feedback may be a lot like the chicken farmer's definition. (Perhaps the only thing worse than a poor feedback process is to achieve goals based on a poorly conceived plan and still fail in the ultimate test of the marketplace!)

Do Not Postpone Facing People Problems

Very early in my career I had to dismiss a young woman who, despite what seemed to be her best efforts, was fouling up almost everything she touched and creating a general disruption in the department as a whole. The first two words out of her mouth when I told her we would have to terminate her employment (after a great deal of agonizing on my part) were, "thank you." She went on to elaborate that she knew she was messing up regularly and felt terrible about it, but she just could not seem to master the job and avoid the errors. By helping her get on with a new job and a new start, I was actually doing a favor to her as well as my company.

Deming Was Wrong About Appraisals

Well known quality authority W. Edwards Deming's intentions were good, but his condemnation of performance appraisals was wrong. Late in his life he was beginning to alter his position on this. Performance planning is an essential part of any management development process, and good management leadership is essential to any business's success. Plans that are tied into the strategic and operating plans of the business can be easily translated into the basis for a good evaluation and performance appraisal. Performance appraisals offer wonderful opportunities for feedback that can lead to improvement and outstanding performance.

They also offer opportunities for miscommunication, poor feedback, no feedback, or incorrect feedback – the last being the worst of all. Many times I have known employees ready to go to their termination meetings who never had really understood that their performances were unacceptable. What a devastating event that must be for that person. Worse yet, the boss doing the firing has known for a long time that the performance of the employee was unacceptable, yet could never quite get around to communicating that it was or how to improve it, even though several verbal and written performance appraisal sessions might have passed. Somehow the boss was just afraid to "hurt the person's feelings" by telling him or her the truth.

This is like a surgeon refusing to remove a diseased organ or repair a medical emergency inside the body for fear of leaving the blemish of an incision. Among the first and most telling questions I ask any company I wish to assess is, How effective is its performance appraisal process and how well is it regarded? Companies who have weak, poorly handled, or mechanical performance appraisals usually have mediocre performance, miscommunication, and confused, disgruntled employees.

I would like to dwell on the topic of fairness. Everybody knows what fairness is – or so it seems. Yet in reality, very few people really understand or are committed to fairness. Some of the basic issues of fairness are what built the labor union movement in America today. Labor unions were created to protect the rights of workers against unfair employers who would take advantage of them at every opportunity. While the good of the company seems to be such a noble cause, it is amazing how many times management takes unfair advantage of their employee subordinates (and often in the name of the "good of the company.") If only they really understood. Taking unfair advantage of employees and treating them unfairly is never in the best interest of the company. In fact, it is usually in the worst interest of the company.

The simplest way to understand this is to think about a time when you were treated unfairly and reflect on how you felt. If the emotion you felt was not outrage or outright despair, it was at least animosity, anger, or disappointment. Most of us spend the majority of our waking lives at work. How pleasant can that be if someone must endure unfair treatment? What constitutes unfair treatment? The answers are so numerous that it is almost impossible to explore them all.

A good example is what I call *looking for loopholes*. A classic example of this, and one that has been attacked both in the courts and with legislation, is the termination of aging or infirm workers to avoid incurring retirement benefits and expensive health care. The whole Employee Retirement Income Security Act (ERISA) legislation was passed to protect one aspect of this type of unfair treatment. The sad thing is that legal protection is both expensive and imperfect. Witness the rash of litigation about sexual discrimination, age discrimination, minority rights abuse, and on and on. How much easier and better would it have been to treat people fairly and not take advantage of them unfairly. Partners act like partners, they do not doublecross each other. Tom Melohn, former owner of North American Tool and Die comments extensively on these principles in his new book, *The New Partnership* [5].

Unions Had a Reason for Existence

Today most of the companies organized by labor unions were organized with one of two purposes in mind: protecting the worker's rights (basic fairness) or greater economic compensation. Would it not have been better for those companies to have dealt with their employees themselves than to have to do so through a third party? It is interesting that some of the labor unions' leaders are often just as good, and forward thinking as management at telling the difference between fair and unfair treatment. Earlier, I went so far as to name a couple of the United Steel Workers "executives" as examples of good union bosses. Not all are good. Many are wrong thinking. Some union leaders have become exactly what unions were formed to overcome – power hungry bullies. They may have been driven to where they are by being victims of untrustworthy management (except for the ones lacking in values and principles who do what they do for personal gain – you see, those traits are not limited to shady "big-business" executives). The point of the preceding sentence is to keep you from deciding that unions are bad or that there can be no partnership if a union is involved. Nothing is further from the truth. In many cases, the management forfeits a lot of its rights by failing to live up to its responsibilities!

As I stated in the introduction, a good definition for a fair deal is one that you would take either side of. You can modify that to say, one that you be willing to live on either side of. For those of you who want it in a little more "down home language," do not sell a horse you would not buy. Just as you could make nothing without materials supplied by your supplier partners, you will not get very far without your employee-associate partners pulling in the direction you want to go.

A happy, informed, involved, and motivated work force can be the greatest competitive weapon in the world. The opposite kind of work force is a ticket on a one-way trip to failure. It will not be a question of if, but when will those employees who are not partners decide to check out physically or mentally, and with them the business will go as well. The sad part about this is that all lose their jobs when that happens and often in such a way that those jobs will never come back (or at least to that town or that part of the country).

Back to Mr. Sam

In Chapter 17 of his autobiography, Sam Walton cites ten rules that worked for him. Considering his earlier statements, it is not surprising that about half of these rules are about his relationships with his associate partners:

Rule 2: Share your profits with all your associates, and treat them as partners. In turn, they will treat you as a partner.

Rule 3: Motivate your partners. Money and ownership aren't enough. Constantly, day by day, think of new and more interesting ways to motivate and challenge your partners ....

Rule 4: Communicate everything you possibly can to your partners. The more they know, the more they'll understand. The more they understand, the more they'll care. Once they care, there's no stopping them. If you don't trust your associates to know what's going on, they'll know you don't really consider them partners.

Another statement I heard recently stuck with me on this topic. Without information, how can anyone really take responsibility for something, and with information, how can anyone not take responsibility?

Mr. Sam's Rules 5, 6, and 7 are also worthy of mention:

Rule 5: Appreciate everything your associates do for the business ....

Rule 6: Celebrate your successes. Find some humor in your failures. Don't take yourself so seriously. Loosen up and everybody around you will loosen up. Have fun ....

Rule 7: Listen to everybody in your company. And figure out ways to get them talking. The folks on the front lines – the ones who actually talk to the customer – are the only ones who really know what's going on out there. You'd better find out what they know.

Find and Support Good People

If it seems like I have cited a lot of Sam Walton – I have. He created a hugely successful enterprise and left a legacy that endures today, in spite of the detractors and nay-sayers. Most important, Mr. Sam grew with his business, he kept learning because he was wise enough to surround himself with bright, talented, highly motivated people and then listen to them and let them operate the company. There are other companies that operate on these kind of principles too – Manco and Jack Kahl, for example – but they are few. Fewer still have been able to grow as Wal*Mart has and still maintain the essence of the culture – the power of partnership with its associates.

One of the most effective ways that Sam Walton continued to build this partnership with his associates is through personal contact and visibility. The term management by wandering around (MBWA) was encountered by many of us in Tom Peters and Bob Waterman's hugely successful book *In Search of Excellence*. It describes the essence of what is needed, but the concept must be taken further. The wandering must be purposeful. It must be planned only to assure that it happens often and productively. In my experience, an executive is easily trapped in an office (or a small group of offices and nearby conference rooms) in meeting after meeting. I know I was guilty of this, and if I was (considering how much I enjoyed and learned from my wandering), then certainly someone who does not realize the importance or feels less than comfortable doing this will avoid it entirely.

Check Your Sources Carefully

Information comes to management in a variety of ways. Some of these are random and incomplete; others are well structured (such as periodic reports). While these are useful (and necessary), they are no substitute for getting out among the first line associates (or customers and suppliers). Information that comes "to the boss" at any level is filtered to remove what the provider feels might be distasteful or reflect poorly on them or their department. This incomplete and filtered (and often biased) information stream is what leads to decisions that are widely perceived as foolish or misdirected. If the people in an organization figure out that they can provide honest, factual feedback without endangering themselves, it will come in both quantity and quality. If the "kill the messenger" approach is used or if the information is directly tied to punishment or retribution, the stream will dry up – forever. To do the right things, it is terribly important to operate on the basis of accurate understanding of the situation. If the information is filtered, distorted, or otherwise unclear, the best intentioned actions can have the opposite effect. When this happens, it polarizes both the associates and the leader. Leaders who thought they were doing the right thing are upset by the bad reaction. The associates' fear that the leader is out of touch with them is confirmed.

Share Information Constantly

The sharing of information is a two-way effort and, as cited earlier in Mr. Sam's rules, requires constant attention. I can recall a situation a few years ago when we were trying to shift the culture at Huffy Bicycles from a plantwide, individual compensation-driven, directive approach to team-based focused factories – quality, service, and productivity driven – with a high-involvement, empowered, and ultimately self-directed team environment. I must have restated the mission and vision hundreds of times (so I thought). Perhaps I did, considering all the constituents I spoke to – from suppliers to customers, associates, and corporate management. What I forgot is that only I heard it and stated it that many times. Some of the groups heard it several times, but not nearly as many as I thought. I was pointedly reminded by an outspoken hourly associate that I needed to restate our mission and vision constantly, until it became "burned into the brain" of everyone (in his words). I once heard Wick Skinner of Harvard put it a way I liked: "the leader must be a 'Johnny one note', constantly restating the vision to the organization."

Constantly and consistently communicating the mission, vision, values, and goals of an organization is but one example of a critical part of building partnerships with employees-associates. Living up to the things that are communicated – walking the talk – is another. The people who make up an organization are constantly looking for either reinforcement or failure to "walk the talk." Trust is based on what they see versus what they hear. A saying I recall states, "Your actions speak so loud I cannot hear your words!" Many good words and deeds can be undone in just a single thoughtless moment. When this happens, the only solution I have found is to admit the "offense" and apologize. (Obviously, correcting the inappropriate action or words is also required, and the sooner the better.)

Once the organization has a clear picture of the larger direction, it becomes necessary to flesh out the skeleton of the direction. Once again, confirmation from the DDI study cites, "The implication of these findings is that high-involvement leadership flourishes best if installed from the top to the bottom of the managerial hierarchy simply because leaders will imitate behaviors of their own leaders." Each smaller subgroup, down to the individual associate, must be helped to understand and find his or her own role in the partnership.

Only when the vision is both shared and owned by a large number of people in the organization can the real power of the partnership begin to take effect. One admonition, it is almost impossible to get everyone to buy in to a given mission, vision, and so on. Perhaps a good saying to keep in mind is, "Anytime you try to please everybody, somebody will not like it!" Another point to remember is that "being a visionary and inspirational leader can be draining, both intellectually and emotionally" [33]. (But take it from someone who has been there, it can be and is stimulating, exhilarating, and intoxicating, too!)

Do Not Lower Your Standards to Get a Buy In

It is critical to get many of the people to buy in, but not at the expense of lowering expectations too greatly. In any organization, there are informal leaders whose involvement is most important. Getting them on board can go a long way toward getting the whole organization moving. While these informal leaders are crucial, some may have their own agenda. This could cause compromises that are undesirable. As in any consensus-driven activity, there is the risk of compromising too much and reaching a lowest common denominator solution that ensures only mediocre goals and results. That is not what partnership is all about! Too often organizations and managers do not "live up" to what they believe in, they "live down" to an easier, compromised set of standards. The fine balance – between sharing the vision, maintaining high goals, and getting widespread buy in – is where the real challenge arises to leaders and participants in building partnerships. Goals, by definition, must be a moving target – always improving, moving up – because competition will be improving too. (An old saying from the bike business seems appropriate here: If we are coasting, we must be going downhill.) The best advice I can give here is that the leaders' values must be strong; and their purposes clear, worthy, and consistent; and their goals and aspirations always reaching higher. Covey's writings discuss this subject as well as anything I have found. I encourage reading one of his three books, *The Seven Habits of Highly Effective People* [1], *Principle Centered Leadership* [45], or *First Things First* [46], to better consider and understand this area.

Values Are Like Beacons in the Darkness

While strong values alone are not sufficient, they are necessary. There will be times when a change in direction is needed, either because the original plans were flawed or the situation has changed. This presents a risk if associates perceive this change as an unethical shift, for some ulterior motive. When fundamental values are strong, and perceived as such, shifts in direction have a much better chance of being explainable and accepted. When the

121

leader's values are strong, the people can sense it like an aura around him or her.

Small Group Meetings Work Best

One of the most effective employee partnership processes I have found is a time-consuming one: frequent small group meetings. These are tiring, often intense, and sometimes perilous sessions. They are also powerful change drivers and vision builders. The open exchange of thoughts and direct answers to questions build a confidence in leadership and an understanding of the business's direction more effectively than most other forms of communication. Even a one-on-one meeting is, perhaps, not as effective because the small group setting prohibits the tendency to make conciliatory comments to one associate and creates multiple reinforcement of what was said (avoiding misquoting and misunderstanding).

A "safety in numbers" effect also allows some things to be raised in a small group that would not come out in a one-to-one session. On the downside, beware the grandstander who wants to walk out of the meeting crowing about how he or she told them so. An associate's own words describe the feeling [33], "Employee motivation and job enjoyment are increased when people have a real part in what they do instead of just being grunts and peons. It takes longer to do special projects with all the participation, but it's made up for by the extra productivity of positive, motivated employees."

Since the grapevine works far faster than most formal communications systems, there is a cumulative knowledge base in the small group meeting process making later groups better informed and more incisive than earlier ones. (Recent developments in e-mail have created what many believe is a new kind of grapevine on the network.)

The effectiveness of small group meetings is one of the factors, I am certain, behind the strong belief by many that plant or location sizes should be limited, if the strongest possible partnership with associates is to be formed. (Imagine the challenge, both physical and logistical, of holding the 40 to 60 meetings required to meet with all of the 2,000 employees, working three shifts at Huffy Bicycles. It was an almost insurmountable problem, which forced us to do it piecemeal, supplemented with larger group meetings of 300 to 500. These sessions are "tolerable" as one-way information delivery vehicles but of limited value for good exchanges of give and take.)

Partnering with the Union

In the process of creating partnerships with employees-associates several special situations merit discussion before we go further. The first of these involves a group of associates represented by a collective bargaining agent, a union. In many cases, management leadership abdicates its role in forming the partnership simply because a union is involved, or because of prior adversary relations with the union (either its rank and file or its leadership). This is a topic I already hit upon twice, but it warrants further attention. While dealing with and through a union alters some of the "rules," it does not (or should not) alter the basic ones – trust, character, active communications, common goals, and so forth are all just as important, and possibly more important, in this situation.

The primary difference is that a corollary partnership with the union leadership must be formed to permit the partnership with the employees to succeed in the best fashion. The union leadership, while theoretically part of the same work force as the rank and file, often has an additional agenda that must be recognized and considered (respected). If this agenda is understood and considered in forming this "subpartnership," then the first step has been taken. Union leaders may feel threatened by a company's aggressive partnership development efforts if they are not involved and informed about the plans, purposes, and expected outcomes. Union leaders who feel threatened will become obstacles to the partnership. On the other hand, those who see the partnership as furthering the prosperity and harmony of the business and organization can find meaningful "self-interest" to motivate their cooperation and support. Once union leaders have achieved a comfort level with management's plans, purposes, and goals for the partnership, they can become powerful allies (which is how things should be).

To be realistic, some unions will not come around, just as some people will not. There are always a small minority of skeptics and cynics. Do not let this stop you. It makes the task of forming a true, effective partnership with hourly associates who are union members much more difficult – but not impossible. Just as there are customers and suppliers who might otherwise be desirable partners that are either unwilling or unable to really "partner," the difficulty should not dampen the enthusiasm for the process.

Partnering Between Functions

In today's fast moving environment most theorists extol the virtues of cross-functional teams. This makes several critical assumptions. The first is that the environment is conducive to teams. The second is that team development is fairly effective. The third is that the cross-functional teams cooperate across the functional boundaries. William Parr and Harland Carothers of the University of Tennessee's Management Development

Center describe the best cross-functional systems approach I have seen [in 16]. Their term *suprasystems* was chosen carefully to signify that these cross-functional systems are more important than the functional silos' activities. When organized around customer-serving roles, some of which they describe as Customer Value Determination, Make, Delivery/Availability, and so forth, the purposes, goals, and objectives of these suprasystems become clearly worthy of everyone's cooperation. These essentially replace the old functional imperatives of Engineering, Marketing, Manufacturing in the delivery of customer value. Cooperation is enhanced because all team and system efforts are directed at recognizing and delivering things that customers value. The functional systems remain as administrative support systems subordinated to the suprasystems. Obviously, no systemic approach can assure that people partner and cooperate, but the closer the system is to the intuitively ideal means of operation, the more likely the people will rally around it.

Councils Are a Form of Internal Partnership

One internal organizational approach that would not normally be thought of as a partnership is what I call a *council*. These were widely used in Rubbermaid to share information and responsibility among the various businesses. For example, the Purchasing Council was one of the most active. This was a group of Purchasing Directors (up or down one managerial level, in some cases) who met regularly as a "council" to compare the programs and pricing they were getting from the various suppliers and plan how to best consolidate the purchasing power and relationships of the corporation to its advantage. One division that was the largest purchaser of a given type of plastic, say PVC, would plan and negotiate the supply, pricing, terms, and so on for the total corporation, and all divisions would buy under that agreement. Obviously, there had to be a lot of information sharing if the "lead division" was to be well informed about the needs of other divisions to do a complete job. At times the council would undertake new initiatives for the corporation, such as new systems or processes, and then take those back to their respective divisions. A senior corporate officer would normally sit in on these sessions as a sort of coordinator, but was really involved in only corporatewide policy or procedure changes. A major side benefit of this kind of partnership was the bond formed between functional counterparts across the entire corporation. A second was that the sharing of ideas among the various divisions filtered back into other functional areas and were used similarly in other divisions or locations. There were R&D councils, Distribution councils, and so forth. The concept of this internal partnership can be extended across almost any part of an organizations. At Huffy, we had a similar, but less effective vehicle called functional meetings. Occasionally these would emulate the councils, but they were more often relegated to information sharing (and less action driven).

One last thought to consider. Few companies succeed equally well at partnerships with all four of the primary partners in all the various dimensions. Simply the process of trying to form partnerships helps in many ways. If some of the relationships evolve to partnerships in a less mature or complete stage, good things can and will happen. *If you recall the brief section on "toughness" at the end of chapter two, it will help you through all kinds of these situations.* One of my former associates liked the term *tough love* to describe how some of these partnerships had to be developed. However it is done, the key is to remember that *it is a true partnership only if there is enough win-win for both partners and it serves the end-user customer!*

If you just finished reading this chapter and said to yourself, "I don't need all that nonsense – I treat the people I deal with fairly most of the time," I challenge you. Do you really, or do you still frame your definition of fairness in that outdated, old-school concept of fairness – being fair when it is convenient? Are you guilty of doing the right thing only when it is easy or when it makes you look or feel good? You need not answer me on this one – just look in the mirror when you get up in the morning and answer yourself.

After all this dialogue about building partnerships with employees and associates, what can and should be done? The real benefits of using books like this are the actions that result. The longer one waits to take action, the greater is the chance that nothing will be done. Because of this, I encourage you to write down the actions that came to mind as you read the chapter. Think about how to build new or better partnerships with employees or associates or how to repair the damage done by errors of the past. It is never too late to get started! In these days of damaged or destroyed feelings of loyalty to employees, a feeling of partnership between employers and employees (associates) is probably the only kind of tie that can bind a person to a company.

Monday Morning List

Five Ways to Improve (two-way) Communication with Employee-Associate Partners:

1. _____

2. _____

3. _____

4. _____

5. _____

Five Aspects of Partnership with Employees or Associates That Should Be Started, Improved, or Repaired:

1. _____

2. _____

3. _____

4. _____

5. _____

Special Professional and Personal Partners

KEY POINTS

- Broaden your horizons to find more partners.
- Arm's length advice can be very valuable (and shocking).
- There is no more need to be vertically integrated in a staffing sense than there is in a manufacturing sense.
- Your tax dollars have already paid for a lot of help – use it.
- Universities can teach more than just their student body – if you are willing to learn.
- Why hire permanently what you need temporarily?
- Swallow your pride and ask for help – local and state governments often respond favorably.
- Students are a valuable resource if used properly.
- Training is the only investment on which the return is infinite.
- You can hire almost anyone, anytime, anywhere these days – just look around.
- Beside every good person is another good person.
- Personal partners are essential to everyone.
- When all else fails – pray. (It works!)
- "Never explain – your friends do not need it and your enemies will not believe you anyway."

In the course of business dealings, we encounter many useful partnering opportunities that do not fall into the categories covered in Chapters 2, 3, and 4. Some relationships may originate with the provider of services being a consultant or advisor in a specific context. Just because these exist, they do not constitute partnerships. A partnership such as this chapter describes usually occurs when a closer, longer term, and more significant working relationship grows between a business and an outside resource. Many of these relationships can be developed into partnerships. From the universe of new partnership forms to be considered, I will list and elaborate on several of the types I have encountered and found successful.

The Professional Partner

The most common professional partnership is usually between a member(s) of management (of the business) and a provider of professional services necessary to conduct or operate the business or to comply with some relevant regulation or law: a lawyer or accountant (or banker). It is fairly normal to build a strong trusting relationship with one or more of these. The more advisory is the role, the more likely and easily a partnership can form. (In the case of a banker, the partnership may be inhibited by the fiduciary responsibility of the banker.)

These advisory partnerships can be among the most valuable because they often provide good quality, arm's length advice within the context of more intimate knowledge of the business and a close (or closer) personal relationship. Top management and often even upper-middle management of a business find difficulty getting objective and informed advice on general business or situational topics (such as alternative competitive strategies). There are numerous consultants, large and small, each offering useful assistance in various specialized areas of the business. Forming "partnerships" with consultants of a traditional nature is a topic unto itself. Joanne Sujansky's book *Power of Partnering* [47] covers this topic in depth. It is worthy of review for those who are involved in extensive (and expensive) consultant partnership efforts. Unfortunately, many of the consultants who deal in specific areas often do not relate to the overall business's strategic or competitive situation. Those who can do this usually are affiliated with large, high-powered (and usually high-priced) firms. Because of this situation, the ability to find the right kind of (affordable and involved) advisor and build a close partnership is an important one. When a high degree of comfort and trust can be built, the partnership can be based upon that trust or comfort platform. Inside information can be shared in confidence. In this case, the advisor becomes informed and familiar with the business's issues, problems, and plans, yet is far enough from the day-to-day pressures to remain objective. This situation creates many opportunities to have a very valuable partner.

The advisor in this kind of a relationship, when it occurs in a general business sense, I call a *retained advisor* (RA). An RA can be, in one context, a "time-shared executive." In another, an RA can bring a specific base of knowhow or experience. The RA can also bring other resources into the partnership, to fulfill needs he or she as the individual or principal RA cannot. (An RA is not the same as an interim executive or a typical consultant in a given specialty who may also provide some general managerial advice.) The needs for an RA might be time constraint driven or brought about by the need for specific experience or professional or technical expertise. In each case, the parallel with medical practitioners calling in specialists to consult or legal specialists retained as advisors comes to mind. There may simply be the need for someone with a broad business experience base with whom the top management can review, discuss, consider, or debate plans.

In some cases, outside directors can perform in such a role, provided they do not feel it compromises their fiduciary responsibility or other requirements of their director's role. Using a director in such an advisory role may not permit management to be as open or honest (direct) as desirable because a legitimate oversight function is performed by this person. Done properly, however, such a partnership can reduce the risk of costly mistakes, increase the speed at which new ventures can be started, or simply validate and contribute to the breadth and depth of the direction being taken.

With the downsizing of many corporations, a significant amount of executive talent is available "for hire." Further, nowhere is it written that companies need to be (fully) vertically integrated in a knowledge sense any more than they are in a production or administrative sense. In fact, both overhead costs and flexibility are enhanced by the use of flexible specialized resources in many areas – why not an experienced, objective, involved and informed retained advisor.

Government Agencies and Public Partners

Lest we limit the horizons of outside support partnerships to consulting or advisory roles, consider two other huge sources of knowledge, information, and potential support: universities and government agencies. Under the right circumstances (refer to the earlier checklist and assessment), these can be some of the most powerful and beneficial partnerships outside the traditional value chain.

Some can even be a form of combined professional and supplier or customer partnership. I had the good fortune to address a unique conference about two years ago. Regional universities and colleges, the U.S. Department of Energy laboratories, consultants, and industrial suppliers were brought together by a large corporation (GM) to share and exchange technology "awareness." The power of such a three- or four-way partnership staggers the imagination. I began to wonder why such collaborations do not happen more often.

Sadly, most such encounters are destined to fail or realize only a small percentage of their potential because the participants are unwilling or unable to find a common basis of understanding on which to communicate. If they do, they still may be too proud to admit that they do not understand how to bridge the gaps between their technological capability or sophistication and the commercial use or feasibility. This area is worthy of much attention and work, especially as the government tries to reduce (and privatize) its spending on defense or aerospace technology.

During the 1960s and 1970s the "space race" provided a use for a great deal of technology – and some of it trickled down to commercial applications. Defense spending is rightfully being curtailed at this time – but how can that knowhow be diverted to commercial purposes? This is very difficult, because the operating culture of a military-defense establishment is very different from those of the for-profit private sector. This difficulty may provide a significantly larger advantage for those companies that figure out how to tap into that technological knowledge base. The previously mentioned Department of Energy laboratories offer this kind of technology base, which is constantly in need of commercialization opportunities. One such lab I am familiar with is located nearby in Oak

Ridge, Tennessee, and continues to spawn numerous entrepreneurial ventures suitable for collaborative partnerships. How many times around the country is this opportunity waiting to be exploited?

Universities often make it even easier than government. The more enlightened ones are actively and intelligently seeking partners in industry. Many have done so for years. They are increasingly realizing (or remembering) that business is the customer for their finished product whether it is an alumnus with an undergraduate (or advanced) degree or an active business person seeking advanced professional education. A few of the more forward thinking MBA programs, such as the one at the University of Tennessee (Knoxville), have made part of the program a "simulation" of the real world of business. The relevance this kind of educational process adds is very valuable to an MBA graduate and especially to the company that hires him or her.

Many universities have been technology partners with companies for years. Small universities like my alma mater, Bradley, have had great partnerships with major corporations (in that case Caterpillar) for decades. Now the better universities (again citing the University of Tennessee as an example) have formed Management Development Centers that not only educate practitioners from industry, but partner with specific companies to perform in a consultative role – a high-value, high-quality, synergistic partnership solution. It is time that the progressive value-maximizing businesses realize that this kind of partnership is one of the "best buys" they can find (before their competitors do). There is no partnership anywhere that cannot be improved on and built further. In far too many cases, the name has been used, but the benefits have not been realized.

Training Partnerships

Another form of industry partnership with higher education or government is in the provision of trained, educated associates with which to build the business. Partnerships, coalitions, and other relationships between local (especially two-year) colleges and universities already exist. The challenge for these programs is to actually produce the right kind and quality of results. Often, neither party spends enough time communicating its situation, and the results are trained people who cannot find jobs because the training was not targeted to local market needs. What a waste of good intentions and public funds. In one of my previous positions a branch campus of an excellent state university was within a few miles of our plant. Even though the plant was always in need of training and education and the branch campus in need of more students, no partnership developed. After many occasions of outlining what educational curriculum would be of value and offering to provide teachers and students, nothing much happened. Why not? Perhaps the administration was so busy being in the educational business, it forgot to be in the business of education. What a waste!

Why Hire Full Time if the Need Is Part Time

An extension of this thought process also leads to another partnership potential: contract or temporary employment firms. In the past few years, I have utilized such a firm and seen just how effective it can be. While at Rubbermaid Office Products, Cobble Personnel, a Knoxville, Tennessee, based firm, provided all of our new hourly associates through the equivalent of their probationary period. Cobble, and similar local and regional firms, can provide a broad range of employees and employment services, from screening through training and beyond. They can even provide interim executives and total contract administrative services (as they do for Navistar's accounting needs). The potential benefit of forming partnerships with such service providers has been recognized for years in many industries but ignored in others. Temporary employment firms can also provide improved labor economics in seasonal situations by taking advantage of counterseasonal employers in their customer base. Rather than continual hiring and layoffs, they can shift employees to different employers. Now is the time to broaden our horizons in looking for ways to stay flexible, keep costs down, and utilize resources and expertise by considering new approaches to partnering.

The Contract Services Partner

This area is so full of possibilities it could fill an entire book itself. Kinko's, the large copy and office-related service centers, is willing to become "contract printing-office service providers," covering a wide range of traditional administrative services. Kinko's is an indispensable partner to many independent and small business people. Partnerships such as these can provide the business user with high-quality services and a broad array of technology with little or no fixed expense for people or equipment. However, many people think these approaches are for the small business only – not so. It can work equally well for small and large alike. As we think about ways to become more flexible and adapt to the changing environment, we must rethink old paradigms about vertical integration of all types, including office administration and even management staffing (not just in the "factory"). Outsourcing of functions that do not fall within the business's core competencies to other, more specialized partners allows all partners to focus on their own areas of expertise.

Local, State, and Federal Partners

The last supporting partnership category I would like to cover (briefly) is with the local, state, and federal governments. In my experience, much press coverage is given to this "partnership" when large plants are sought after by states and the dollar sums often provided in both economic and service benefits are staggering. What is largely ignored is the day-to-day support many states, counties, and cities could or do provide to companies for staying home and expanding. I have had firsthand experience in start-ups (in Oklahoma), expansions (in Ohio and Tennessee), and plant site searches (in the Carolinas). Once the decision to locate or expand in a given area has been made, the true partnership with the government or industrial development agencies can really begin. Since all parties involved want the venture to be a success, there is an immediate mutual self-interest. This self-interest can bind the partnership together and make it very successful. Once again the resources are funded with tax dollars that someone will get and spend – why not your company? Training, employment services, and technology support are just a few of the special services that can be provided by a government industrial development partner.

State industrial development functions appear to have a predisposition toward finding new employers. Seldom do they "forage" as hard for ways to help existing employers grow and expand. Neither do the existing industries devote as much time and effort as they should to gain this attention. Like the well-documented "lifetime value of a customer," it seems obvious that it should be easier to grow the existing or established base of business than fight for the hard-to-win new ones. (These fights are often expensive and can not only damage existing employers by their terms, but also present many opportunities for a public economic loss!) Neither do the expansion plans for existing plants gain the publicity that new locations do – why?

The purpose of industrial development is, quite simply, to increase employment thus increasing the prosperity and tax base of the locale involved. It seems to me that this is an entirely capitalistic (and valid) motive. Very often, existing (and unsophisticated new) companies fail to even explore this source of help. With no new plant start-up or a life-or-death situation, the prevailing lack of awareness of many small or mid-size companies about how to tap this resource may explain why such partnerships are not formed more often. Large companies may have special functions whose existence depend on gaining continuing tax relief, but there is much more to a partnership than simply the money one partner can provide. The ability to network into resources from other branches of government is becoming increasingly "worth the red tape." This area of industrial development is one of the richest ones to explore for new partnership forms and benefits.

Venture Capital and Investor Partners

Supporting partners can come from many other places. The ones described here are only the largest or most obvious opportunities. Actively seek out partners! Some banks have functions that sponsor and help small start-up businesses in hopes of developing a larger client in the future. Venture capital firms can also become a partner in the right context. Money managers are always searching for places to invest their funds, and they can help in more than just financing, by bringing together partners that complement each other. The World Bank is a rich source of funds for international projects that meet its criteria. Do not forget the masses of merchant bankers, deal makers, and similar service providers that are now available in every imaginable industrial or economic field.

Private Foundation Partners

Private foundations have billions of dollars they are commissioned to grant to further the purposes outlined by their charter or mission. Some organizations have become specialists at tapping into this kind of funding, year after year, forming a de facto partnership even if it is dependency based (a less than ideal form of partnership because it is "lopsided," favoring one partner over the other). To be successful in developing partnerships in this particular area, a base of expertise must be developed. The proposal process, once properly developed, improves the probability of success (assuming the need for the funding is legitimate and within the intent of the foundation). A good approach to foundations with worthy causes for needed funds can usually be applied across many foundations. The only way to get started (as in many partnerships, getting started is the hardest part) is to just do it and learn from the experience.

Horizons Are Unlimited, Search Everywhere

How does one go about finding, considering, and making contact with all the potential partners discussed in this chapter? Start with your local Chamber of Commerce, county and state Department of Development, and college or university. Do not ignore the community or two-year colleges. They are receiving increased shares of state funding because their enrollment is rising while four-year schools' enrollment has flattened out or declined – and their capabilities are growing along with their size and student base. The public library is one of the most overlooked sources of research information, and one that can be used easily and inexpensively. The Internet and World Wide Web opens an entire new range of possibilities, far too broad for discussion in this book, but certainly worthy of mention as perhaps the information and contact source of the twenty-first century.

An Unusual Partner – a Competitor!

One type of partnership usually forgotten in any discussion of partnerships is the joining of forces of either cooperating or competing companies to achieve a given objective. Consider for a moment the partnership between Coca-Cola and McDonald's. There is a supplier-customer relationship. There is also a cross-promotional partnership. Cross-promotional partnerships take many forms. Using one company's product in another's is a common one. Oreo cookies from Nabisco show up in TCBY stores with their yogurt dishes all over the country. Gas stations often tie in with sports teams, soft drink companies, and many others in their promotions. At Huffy Bicycles, we had an excellent partnership with Procter and Gamble to use bikes as promotional items either to sell more of their products or as sales contest and in-store incentives. There is a limitless universe of potential tie-ins – not limited even by competing companies.

The manuscript for this book was done on an Apple Macintosh Powerbook, because it is simply a more user-friendly computer than IBM or its clones, even with Windows. Now IBM and Apple are talking about forming a partnership to make their products more compatible and even to use them intermingled. Microsoft's Word for Windows has grown in popularity because it will "read" many different word processing software programs' output. Is this a revolutionary kind of partnership? Sprint,

MCI or AT&T and the various Baby Bells are not sure whether to partner or fight – but partnering is much the better option if they can work it out. As previously mentioned, the partnering among telephone, cable, cellular phone, TV, and other electronic media is creating a new universe of possibilities. How many new types of partnerships can we imagine? A limitless number. But, they all fall under the same set of rules and criteria for success, in varying measures. Go back to the early chapters and refer to the checklists, assessments, and processes. They are applicable almost universally.

The Personal Partners

Let me go on to a more subtle, and perhaps more important, partnership that is often overlooked, but seldom absent in the life of any successful person. This is the personal partner. The personal partner may be one person or several, depending on the situation. Before there were so many successful female managers and executives, an old cliché was very true: Behind every successful man is a good woman. I am not sure how to restate this for the 1990s, but I will give it a try: Beside every successful person, there is a good, supporting partner (or perhaps, "around every successful person is a network of partnerships").

Somehow, it loses a little of the old time flavor, but it is just as surely true. Perhaps the most obvious example is the highest executive office in our government. Is there any doubt that the resident of 1600 Pennsylvania Avenue, currently a Mr. Clinton, depends greatly on his partner? Many previous chief executives of the United States have similarly relied on their partners to provide them advice, solace, objectivity, and support in times of trouble. (Perhaps few have had so public a partner in the business of government, but many have had very influential spouses, going back to Eleanor Roosevelt and up to Nancy Reagan and Barbara Bush.)

Too often, people in general and especially executives and managers try to insulate or isolate their spouses (or families) from the problems at work. They surely affect their relationships and home lives with the (work-related) stress induced behavior, but they do not take advantage of one of the most natural of partnerships. The motives for not sharing business issues with a spouse (or family) and not seeking partnership or support may differ in each case – some may be good, others bad. In either case the result is to deny access to a supportive and complementary thought process. (Most marriages, according to popular psychologists, are formed of complementary personality types that tend to "complete" the respective partners.)

In my personal experience, my spouse has brought objectivity, love, concern, and especially a fresh, empathetic viewpoint to many issues I faced. As in all partnerships, to gain the return, an investment (of trust) must be made. I trust her and must share my experiences, feelings, and problems with her if she is to help.

On the checklist of partnership criteria, many of the prerequisites should be easily met (remember that a good partnership has many of the same attributes of a marriage). If this is the case, then build that partnership by sharing information (one of the other partnership prerequisites) so your partner can help you. Often the help needed is, at first, a sympathetic ear. Sometimes, just telling someone about a problem reveals the solution! If the information sharing is not too biased (always a potential problem), there is a chance for some caring, objective feedback. Defensive behavior is poison to any relationship because it blocks open information exchange and builds walls of resistance, so the same applies here. It almost seems that this section might have gone first, doesn't it. There are far too many good books on the market about the dynamics of a good marriage relationship for me to do much more here than remind you of this powerful, sensitive, and ideally supporting partnership. Once again, I refer the reader to Stephen Covey's books for additional insights into these kinds of partnerships.

In many cases, the next partnership most easily built and enjoyed is between parent and child. This one can work either direction. For many years, the parent counsels the child in the ways of the world and life in general. This can continue in a business situation providing the two partners are willing. (Remember the discussion about willingness to form the partnership in Chapter 1?) Once the desire is there, the rules are not very different. Since there is by definition a "generation gap" in this case, both benefits and disadvantages exist. The benefits are derived from the two different social perspectives that will be brought to the partnership. Even though the process of raising a child instills many of the parents' values, the time spent as an individual building one's own character and values will bring a very different perspective in most cases.

The values derived from the formative years (birth–12) of the two individuals are necessarily different. This provides a somewhat risky basis for objective differences. Only if the parent will accept the relative equality in the value of the two partners' input can this partnership maximize its potential. It is important here to recall how the viewpoints and values of individuals are shaped by the period of history in which they grew up. Each generation's experiences dramatically influence perceptions, beliefs, and values and cannot be overlooked. I can recall numerous cases where I gained important insights into my own problems while sharing some of my concerns with my three children as they grew up.

Consider for a moment more the difference in values brought about by the period when one grew up. Depression children, born in the late 1920s and early 1930s, now in their 60s or older, were painfully aware of the lack of jobs, threats to economic security, and so forth; and their values would favor these things they saw lacking during their formative years. Those born later and growing up in the turbulent 1960s assign importance to different sets of values. Living through a period of rebellion (socially) and almost unlimited growth (economically) has given them a much different outlook on life. They are much more concerned about society and its ills than the issue of personal security. Any given decade's "children" will have many of their values shaped by that time's crises and cultural shifts. While many core values will be the same, many others will be very different. When attempting to forge a good partnership with anyone of a different generation, and especially a parent-child partnership, there must be a deep appreciation of the value differences. These differences are a source of fresh viewpoints if they are appreciated as such. In partnerships, diversity of viewpoint is one of the important synergies gained – but only if the partners are receptive to the diversity of opinions that result and have respect for their partners' opinions and viewpoints.

Another important personal partnership has a religious and moral base. It may be with clergy or it may be from a deep sense of personal religious beliefs. This partnership can be a wellspring of strength during difficult times. One often senses that the things one is doing are right (or wrong) either ethically or morally. Having the principles, character, and courage to accept that belief, without fully understanding where it comes from, is the mark of a person who has found this very special partnership. Stephen Covey, in his writings, covers this subject in several different ways. These books are excellent references for anyone who wishes to further understand and reflect on how to build a stronger partnership in a moral or spiritual sense.

Covey's term *principle centered leadership* is a good one. Others have used the term a *sense of purpose*. Whatever set of words you choose, the most important thing is that you find your own way of internalizing the feeling and using it to find a partner who can reinforce it when needed. A clergy confidant can be a resource in a personal sense and also an objective sounding board for the ideas, wishes, and hopes not often shared with anyone else. Religion and religious beliefs form a foundation for dealing with some of life's most difficult situations.

To wrap up this chapter, list the ten best professional partnerships you have or might have and the three most important personal partnerships that influence your life. Then think about how you can make them even stronger.

__Monday Morning List__

Ten Best Professional Partnerships:

1. _____
2. _____
3. _____
4. _____
5. _____
6. _____
7. _____
8. _____
9. _____
10. _____

Three Best Personal Partnerships:

1. _____
2. _____
3. _____

Partnership-Based Reconfiguration

KEY POINTS

- Change is the only constant in these turbulent times.
- Business is becoming more complex, with rising levels of unpredictability.
- Linear extrapolation of the past will not predict the future.
- There are no "magic pills" for business success.
- If American managers could read themselves to world dominance we would certainly have succeeded.
- An integrative solution is needed to utilize all the piecemeal approaches and programs managers have learned over the past two decades.
- Industries, leaders, and executives must transform themselves.
- The ability to build partnerships around core competencies that deliver value will be the basis for competitive advantage.
- Top managers must be leaders and strategic architects, with the curiosity, imagination, and technical competence to evolve their core competencies to those that will be valued.
- The battle for dominant global position in markets will go to the swiftest, only if they can swiftly adapt to what customers will value in the future.

"The times they are a-changin'!" goes the old saying. This seems more true than ever as we reach the mid-point of the 1990s. Dealing with ever-accelerating rates of change in society, technology, business, and competition requires an integrative approach, not the disjointed, piecemeal way things have been done for the past 20 to 30 years.

Over the past two decades many excellent approaches have been developed to help achieve the goal of most businesses – creating a sustainable competitive advantage that can be converted into superior economic returns for their owners or stakeholders. Many of these have been re-applications of old U.S. techniques and approaches that were used against U.S. industries by the Japanese (and renamed in Japanese words). Often these were little more than contemporary adaptions of basic techniques long known, used, and then forgotten in the demand-driven frenzy of the 1960s and early 1970s.

Some were genuinely based on new and improved understanding of how to succeed in a different, more rapidly changing competitive environment. The names and acronyms are well known to most modern managers and executives: quality circles, JIT, CIM, employee involvement, participative management, activity-based costing/measurement, MRP, the theory of constraints, TQM, QFD, Kaizen, competing-in-time, lean production, strategic alliances, category management, EDI, VMR, QR, agile manufacturing, reengineering, and many, many more.

These approaches (I refer to them as *approaches* because they varied widely in scope and execution) each dealt with a single (or multi-dimensional) *part* of the entire enterprise. Some were useful primarily in manufacturing; others in quality, accounting, or sales. Some applied to business processes or activities across several disciplines. What none of them did was *create a complete integrative basis for the strategy or its execution* in the business's overall context. Perhaps this was because, until fairly recently, few contemporary management strategists understood or accepted the role of manufacturing or operations as a key contributor of strategic advantage. Perhaps it was because it is usually easier to fix a part of something than the whole thing. The field of logistics and the concept of lean production has, perhaps, come the closest to dealing with an integrated thought process. Because logistics deals with the complete supply chain management, it has yielded some great benefits. Writing in the *MDC Update* of the University of Tennessee's College of Business, Thomas Greenwood [48] discusses a large part of the integration. He says: "the first redesign activity in lean production implementations is to reduce manufacturing throughput times and improve product quality by creating flow manufacturing processes.... The second initiative is to extend the capabilities of flow manufacturing in both directions of the value chain to where the largest opportunities exist...forward to customer order management and back through the material supply channels."

He is on the right track – but he needs to go further than that and in more, different directions. Only when the entire network of partners is integrated will the enterprise (or business, if you prefer) be able to develop a competitive strategy for delivering the maximum customer value compared to all competitors. Many of the named "approaches" yielded some advantage for their users when competitors had not yet successfully improved that portion of their business. The ability to create sustainable competitive advantage is no longer dependent on any single type of "improvement," since the conditions in the environment are not static – they are constantly changing. What creates the competitive advantage today may be ineffective next month, or next year, because the environment, technology, market, or competition has changed.

In an article on "value disciplines", Michael Treacy [49] contends that being good at one of the disciplines (he names three: customer intimacy, product leadership, and operating excellence) was sufficient to compete in the past. He contends that now being good at (even) two is not enough. To compete in the 1990s and beyond, a business must be superior at one value discipline and good at the other two. Another way to say it is that improved competitors simply keep "raising the stakes" to compete successfully.

The Race to Reconfigure

Alvin Toffler, the noted futurist describes it this way.

Our corporations are dealing with the trauma of trying to adjust – an attempt by dinosaurs to become micro-dinosaurs – often without making the fundamental changes necessary to adapt to the new realities. Business is becoming more complex, with rising levels of unpredictability. Predictions tend to be based on linear extrapolation – the notion that current trends predict the future. The problem is, trends don't consider the overall context and what else is happening at any given time. Surprises and upsets can and do occur – particularly in periods of upheaval.

The approach I refer to as reconfiguration builds on the power of partnerships to do exactly what Toffler describes as needed – it adjusts. In fact, the linkages between partners enable the reconfiguration of the business. The business with its four major types of partners adjusts in such a way as to utilize the core competencies and capabilities of the organization and adapt them to the constantly changing external competitive environment – and its "upsets."

The partnerships allow the business to reconfigure itself in four dimensions:

- It can restructure, changing its form (to meet new markets, competitors, etc.).

- It can reengineer, dramatically simplifying how things are done (often improving cost and speed, within its form).

- The business can utilize principles of TQM and participation to effectively create a learning organization (which is both highly effective and very adaptive in doing whatever is needed).

- Finally, it can build on the alliances and partnerships to assure that all parts of its extended organization can respond to change in unity (not in disarray or chaos, as so often happens).

By using these four dimensions the business can influence and continually adapt to attain the six attributes of reconfiguration.

These six attributes are the external manifestation of things done right and right things done to yield competitive advantage: *quality, service, cost, time-speed, innovation,* and (the ultimate one) *value.* These attributes are more specific and measurable than Treacy's value disciplines and therefore should be more readily understood and used. With a clear understanding of what mix of these attributes the customers value, all the resources of an enterprise can be aligned and exploited for maximum competitive advantage. The proper mix of these attributes is what the customer value determination process previously mentioned seeks to find [50]. But, to attempt to deliver the mix of attributes without first creating the enabling partnerships and a learning organization will lead to chaos, disarray, and failure.

Partnerships Enable Reconfiguration

Creating partnerships alone does not ensure success. If a business has weaknesses in several critical areas, no amount of partnerships and "reconfiguration" will guarantee its success. It might, however buy time to rectify some of the problems or build the necessary skills, competencies, organization, structure, and talent to allow it to succeed eventually. I must clarify another semantics issue here, lest the reader misunderstand similar terminology.

The term enterprise integration (EI) has been used several places in current literature. Most recently I have seen it well described in John Sheridan's *Industry Week* article "EI: The Next Plateau" [51]. His synopsis is worth repeating here to clarify that this is not the same kind of integration I am referring to. They are complementary, but different! Sheridan writes: "The basic premise of enterprise integration is easy enough – using information technology to link people, business functions, activities, and locations into a seamless web. The tough part is coping with an endless series of options and technical issues."

Just as partnering must deal with complex people issues, this supporting technology called EI struggles with the options and technical issues. I do not want to minimize how useful and important EI can be to the success of partnerships. It is possible to achieve partnerships without EI, but that makes the process much tougher because inadequate or untimely information can cause issues to arise when none should. Partnership is tough enough to achieve without any other obstacles to contend with. Because of this, enlightened top management must understand the importance of investing in good, up-to-date information technology.

To best understand what reconfiguration based on partnerships is all about, look at Figure 6.1. The diagram helps illustrate the dimensions and attributes. The four bold titles at the "points of the compass" mark the *four dimensions* of reconfiguration, and the six italicized words that "surround" the compass are the *six attributes* of reconfiguration. In the center of any reconfiguration-based strategy are the core competencies and capabilities of the organization [52, 53].

Note carefully that I ascribed the competencies and capabilities to the organization, which is made up of people working in a prescribed manner and relationship with each other. Nothing other than their employment agreements, the necessary funding, and their inter-dependent environment ties this set of competencies and capabilities to any given business entity. To expand on the subject of where the core competencies and capabilities reside, the impact of reconfiguration and organization flexibility goes far beyond the range of this book. Hence, it will be reserved for a future one. (It is a pivotal issue for the future.)

Around the periphery of the hexagon, the value attributes of a highly functioning organization are shown. These are the attributes that create competitive advantage with the ultimate customer or end user compared to an alternative competitor. These six value attributes measure, deliver, and testify to the success of the various dimensions of reconfiguration.

The dimensions are separated into four discrete group-ings. Two of them deal with structure and processes, the other two deal with the interaction of people and organiza-tions. It is an indisputable fact that there is a vital link between structure, processes, and how people in organiza-tions perform. Much of the attention in management writ-ing has been given to three of the four dimensions. This work is widely available and will not be discussed at length except to tie together the whole concept of reconfig-uration. The dimension that has been ignored, given lip service but little substantive exploration, is the one of partnerships (and alliances, which are a related but a dif-ferent alternative, useful in the proper situation). I have devoted considerable space to describing the partnerships that are, in fact, the cornerstones. These are the key miss-ing element in making reconfiguration possible and power-ful.

The Integrative Approach

Whether in business or in competitive sports, the structure and processes used can either enhance or detract from the performance of the people and organization and vice-versa. In fact, some may dispute the words or acronyms used to describe these in Figure 6.1. Indeed, they are not pure or indisputable, because in their broad-est interpretation, they too are all blends (TQM is surely not just about the interaction among people – it is very much about processes – but its primary focus is a people-process one).

The real essence and power of partnership-based reconfiguration is perhaps best described in a competitive sports analogy, that of American football. The coach and general manager seek, recruit, hire, and train talent. This is the way businesses also proceed. A "system" is installed,

FIGURE 6.1
Integrative Approach
The Dimensions and Attributes of Reconfiguration

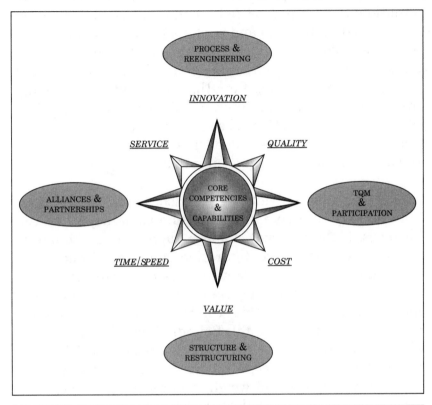

which is analogous to the structure (or restructure). Within the system, the coach develops a play book, which consists of plays (processes, perhaps reengineered ones) that capitalize on the talent of the players (core competencies and capabilities). There are assistant coaches, often dealing in a wide variety of disciplines from strength and conditioning to execution of specific plays (functions). This complement of coaches, players, and supporting systems makes up the partnerships and participation elements.

When all of the ingredients of the team and its play book have been brought together, game plans are developed. These game plans must fit the specific competitive situation: the competitor, field conditions, personnel situation (including injuries and mishaps). This is analogous to a business plan for a given market, time-frame, and so on. *As soon as the competition begins, circumstances start changing.* It is precisely then that the ability to "reconfigure" makes the critical difference. Just as the game plan, play selection, and talent used are adjusted to competition and conditions, so too is the business reconfigured to meet the needs of the competitive situation.

Each of the individual "approaches" discussed earlier may be very effective and fine-tune some aspect of the business. If the external changes happen to match one of them, an effective reconfiguration can occur. None takes fully into consideration the whole business interaction, the strategy and tactics, and the dynamic external environment. (An exception to this statement is the suprasystems concept presented by Stahl, Bounds, Carrothers, Parr, et. al. [16].) Partnership-based reconfiguration does! It is an integrative way to recognize the attributes that lead to competitive success and weigh the proper balance of each *dimension* to maximize the effect on the most important *attributes* in each competitive situation. It does not replace or make obsolete any of the other programs, processes, or "approaches" everyone has so diligently pursued in hopes of elusive success. (Assuming they were done reasonably correctly.) Rather it integrates them and focuses them on the competitor and the situation. It also does so efficiently – requiring no adjustment in areas that will not affect the competitive outcome very greatly. Because partnership-based reconfiguration builds on all the prior investments, it is the ideal integrative culmination. It not only uses prior investments (instead of wasting them as some "programs or approaches" do), but it also leverages them to your benefit.

Partnership-based reconfiguration combines very well with the suprasystems (core business systems) concepts advanced by Stahl, Bounds, Carothers, Parr, et. al. [16] and discussed earlier in several places. It develops the systematic evaluation of how to use all of the leverage of its *dimensions* in combination with the core competencies and capabilities of the organization to achieve the proper balance of *attributes* needed to build and maintain a competitive advantage in customer value delivery in the face of constantly changing external conditions and competition. Above all else, an integrative, systemic approach is the key ingredient in achieving success. No amount of perfection of subordinate approaches (such as TQM or reengineering) will provide success if the strategy of the business toward providing customer value is not correct. The entire concept of customer value determination and delivery [50] is being developed further at this very time by the University of Tennessee and will be explored further in a future work on that topic and one on reconfiguration.

The New Shape Shifters?

Certainly, by the time you have finished reading this, the world will have changed. New names for "new approaches" will be appearing: the lean enterprise, agile competition, the extended organization, genetic diversity, coalition building (are not coalitions really partnerships?), and many more. Already, since this manuscript was in preparation the new book *Competing for the Future* by Gary Hamel and C. K. Prahalad [54] came out. In this, they extol the virtues of "getting to the future first." Their views have created a considerable stir because they seem so right. What they do not describe in as much detail is "how." Because of this, my next book will attempt deal specifically with the "how" and explain how partnership-based reconfiguration copes with these changes.

Two main thoughts to drive home here are that *partnerships are the enabling cornerstones upon which the necessary changes in architecture are built and companies must become "shape shifters" to succeed in the change-driven competition of the twenty-first century half of this decade.* The name and concept of a "Shape Shifter" comes from a character on *Star Trek – The Next Generation*© who assumed the shape most compatible with and conducive to what he hoped to achieve! This capability, and the associated behaviors and practices, will be even more imperative in the 10 to 15 years that are to come after the turn of the century. The job of managing and leading in the remainder of the twentieth century will be surpassed only by the market and customer demands of the twenty-first century. The jobs of followers will be equally demanding, because the rate of change may often exceed the rate at which information from their leaders is being disseminated to them.

Everyone in an organization plays an important role in the transformation of a business. Each person must understand the system architecture that is planned and prepare to contribute to the success of the enterprise. Only senior management leaders can create "hope," but everyone can spread the "infection" of positive, enthusiastic cooperation with their partners. Learning organizations will be the winners in the future. They are the ones who can adapt most quickly, provided they understand enough about the plans, goals, architecture, and strategies devised by their leadership.

In my experience, any time the rate of change exceeded the rate of learning, chaos resulted. This makes it imperative that we spread the practice and development of learning organizations from top to bottom of our organizations. Once this is well underway, the formation of partnerships becomes much easier and more effective. Only if the partnerships have been formed, the advance work done, and these cornerstones set in place can the enterprise win the "race to reconfigure" (or in the Star Trek idiom, become the *new shape shifters*), constantly reshaping themselves to deliver what the customer will value "next," as well as what is valued now.

The future belongs to the swift, the nimble, the competent, and the "best value" provider. Single-mindedness of purpose is essential in the relentless pursuit of these four key partnerships, the cornerstones for the systems architecture, and the delivery of customer value. I almost fear putting this admonition at the end of the book, because most contemporary business people lack the persistence to finish a business book – even one as short as this. I hope those that do will seriously consider this statement.

Writing in a "too little read" working paper almost ten years ago, Duncan McDougall [55] of Boston University said it as clearly as I feel it now: "But I have my doubts as to the willingness and ability of American corporations to adopt and pursue strategically critical purposes with persistence."

If you have read this far, you are far more persistent than most. I hope you will do your part to put the foundation cornerstones of partnerships in place in your business or organization. Make dynamic partnership-based reconfiguration possible to "shift your shape" for the delivery of customer value. This will be your most powerful strategy for the future decades.

I would like to hear from those of you who successfully use partnerships (or reconfiguration) to advance your business – write to share your success stories (and, if they are not successes, those are of interest, too) and send them along. You see, this is not the "end," it is really just the beginning – of the future!

See you in the future! Want to race and see who gets there first? And in what "shape"?

Bibliography

References

[1] Covey, Stephen R. *The Seven Habits of Highly Effective People.* New York: Simon and Schuster, 1989.

[2] Peters, Thomas J., and Waterman, Robert H. *In Search of Excellence.* New York: Harper and Row, 1982.

[3] —"Partnerships: Creating Synergy." Training materials for the course Strategies for High-Involvement Leadership. Pittsburgh: Developmental Dimensions International, 1994.

[4] Levitt, Theodore. *The Marketing Imagination.* New York: The Free Press, 1983. 5.

[5] Melohn, Tom. *The New Partnership.* Essex Junction, NH: Omneo, an imprint of Oliver Wight Publications, 1994.

[6] Senge, Peter. *The Fifth Discipline.* New York: Doubleday Books, 1990.

[7] Barber, James C. "From the Working Class to the Learning Class." *National Productivity Review* (Autumn 1994): 461–466.

[8] —Where Are the New Rules? *Industry Week* (February 3, 1992): 27–30.

[9] —"View From The Top: John Mariotti Speaks Out." *TEI Newsletter* (July–August 1990).

[10] —"How a U.S. Manufacturer Is Beating Very Tough Foreign Competition." John L. Mariotti in *Boardroom Reports* (March 1, 1988).

[11] Dumaine, Brian. "Mr. Learning Organization." *Fortune* (October 17, 1994): 147–157.

[12] Shelton, Ken. "Partners: Worth Their Weight in Gold." *Executive Excellence* 10, no. 11 (November 1993): 2.

[13] Godfrey, A. Blanton. "Ten Clear Trends for the Next Ten Years." In *Profiting from Total Quality*. New York: The Conference Board, 1993. 10–11.

[14] Blackwood, Francy. "Strategic Partnerships, Survival in the Ninties." *HFD* (September 27, 1993): 1–6.

[15] Schmitt, Wolfgang. "The Ethics of Partnerships." *Executive Excellence* 10, no. 11 (November 1993). 15.

[16] Stahl, Michael, and Bounds, Gregory. *Competing Globally Through Customer Value*. New York: Quorum Books, 1991.

[17] Kahl, Jack. "The Ethics of Partnership." *Duck Tales* (November–December 1993).

[18] Fisher, Roger, and Ury, William. *Getting to Yes*. New York: Houghton Mifflin, 1981.

[19] Hamel, Gary, and Prahalad, C. K. "Strategic Intent." *Harvard Business Review* (May–June 1989). 63–76

[20] Sheridan, John H. "Are You a Bad Customer?" *Industry Week* (August 19, 1991): 24–34.

[21] Rockey, Bob. "Strategic Partnerships." *Executive Excellence* 10, no. 11 (November 1993). 20.

[22] Champy, James. "What Comes After Business Reengineering?" *Index SMI Review* (Fourth Quarter 1993): 8–9.

[23] Womack, James, and Jones, Daniel. "From Lean Production to the Lean Enterprise." *Harvard Business Review* (March–April 1993): 93–103.

[24] —"Agile Competitive Behavior – Examples from Industry." Agile Manufacturing Enterprise Forum, Working Papers (July 1994).

[25] —"Twenty-first Century Manufacturing Enterprise Strategy." An Industry Led View, vol. 1. Bethlehem, PA: Iacocca Institute, Lehigh University, 1991.

[26] Bottoms, David. "Back to the Future, Revisiting the Promise of the 'Virtual Corporation'." *Industry Week* (October 3, 1994): 61–65.

[27] Lewis, Jordan. *Partnerships for Profit: Structuring and Managing Strategic Alliances.* New York: The Free Press, 1990.

[28] Guaspari, John. "Had Any 'Value Conversations' Lately?" *Leadership Report* [Rath and Strong] (Spring 1994): 3–5.

[29] Treece, James B., Shiller, Zachary and Kelly, Kevin. "Hardball Is Still GM's Game." *Business Week* (August 8, 1994): 26.

[30] Womack, James P., Jones, Daniel T., and Roos, Daniel. *The Machine That Changed the World.* New York: Rawson division of Macmillan, 1990.

[31] Shewmaker, Jack. "Partnership in the 90's." Presentation to the International Mass Retailers Association convention, 1990.

[32] Serwer, Andrew E. "McDonald's Conquers the World." *Fortune* (October 17, 1994): 103–116.

[33] Howard, Ann, and Wellins, Richard. *High-Involvement Leadership – Changing Roles or Changing Times.* Pittsburgh: Development Dimensions International and Leadership Research Institute, 1994.

[34] Coker, Pamela. "Let Customers Know You 'Love' Them." *Nation's Business* (1993). 9.

[35] —"Prosperity." *Industry Week* (March 19, 1990).

[36] Moody, Patricia E. "Best Customer, the Other Side of the Fence." *AME Target* (Fall 1991): 17–22.

[37] Peters, Thomas J. *Liberation Management.* New York: Alfred A. Knopf, 1992.

[38] Naisbitt, John. *Global Paradox*, New York: Avon Books, 1994. 61-86.

[39] Arlen, Jeffrey. "Cyber Trust: Will It Work?" *Discount Store News* (July 1994). A12–A14.

[40] —"Some Cool Thoughts for Hot Summer Days." *Inside Retailing* (June 20, 1994).

[41] Henkoff, Ronald. "Service Is Everybody's Business." *Fortune* (June 27, 1994): 48–60.

[42] Handy, Charles. *The Age of Paradox*. London: Random House, 1994.

[43] Walton, Sam, with John Huey. *Made in America, My Story*. New York: Doubleday Books, 1992.

[44] Sonnenberg, Frank K. "Managing with a Conscience." *Industry Week* (August 16, 1993).

[45] Covey, Stephen R. *Principle Centered Leadership*. New York: Simon and Schuster, 1990.

[46] Covey, Stephen R. *First Things First*. New York: Simon and Schuster, 1994.

[47] Sujansky, Joanne G. *Power of Partnering: Vision, Commitment, and Action*. San Diego, CA: Pfeiffer and Co. 1991.

[48] Greenwood, Thomas G. "Lean Production Systems: A Blueprint for Reengineering Business Processes." *MDC Update* [Management Development Center, University of Tennessee, College of Business Administration] (Fall 1993): 1–6.

[49] Treacy, Michael, and Wiersma, Fred. "Customer Intimacy and Other Value Disciplines." *Harvard Business Review* (January–February 1993): 84–93.

[50] Gardial, Sarah. "Understanding Customer Value and Satisfaction." Presented at University of Tennessee Senior Executive Institute on Productivity Through Quality, 1994.

[51] Sheridan, John H. "EI: The Next Plateau." *Industry Week* (June 20, 1994): 30–38.

[52] Prahalad, C. K., and Hamel, Gary. "The Core Competence of the Corporation." *Harvard Business Review* (May–June 1990): 79–91.

[53] Stalk, George, Evans, Philip, and Shulman, Lawrence E. "Competing on Capabilities: The New Rules of Corporate Strategy." *Harvard Business Review* (March–April 1992): 57–69.

[54] Hamel, Gary, and Prahalad, C. K. *Competing for the Future*. Boston: Harvard Business School Press, 1994.

[55] McDougall, Duncan C. "The Principle of Slack Ropes or Managing on Purpose." School of Management Working Paper Series, Boston University (October 9, 1986).

Recommended Further Reading

Blackwell, Roger. From the Edge of the World. Columbus: Ohio State University Press, 1994

Drucker, Peter F. "The Five Deadly Business Sins." *The Wall Street Journal* (October 21, 1993).

Drucker, Peter F. *Managing for Turbulent Times*. New York: Harper and Row, 1980.

Ghemawat, Pankaj. "Sustainable Advantage." *Harvard Business Review*. (September–October 1986): 53–58.

Hamel, Gary, and Prahalad, C. K. "Strategy as stretch and Leverage." *Harvard Business Review* (March–April 1993): 75–84.

Hammer, Michael. "Reengineering Work: Don't Automate, Obliterate." *Harvard Business Review* (July–August 1990): 104–112.

Hammer, Michael, and Champy, James. *Reengineering the Corporation*. New York: HarperCollins Books, 1993.

—"Low Wages No Longer Give Competitive Edge." *The Wall Street Journal* (March 16, 1988).

Maurer, Rick. *Caught in the Middle*. Cambridge, MA: Productivity Press, 1992.

Miller, James B. *The Corporate Coach*. St. Martin's Press, New York: 1993.

—"A Practical Guide to Alliances: Leapfrogging the Learning Curve – A Perspective for U.S. Companies." Viewpoint [Booz-Allen and Hamilton] (1993).

Peters, Tom. *Thriving on Chaos*. New York: Alfred A. Knopf, 1987.

Stalk, George, Jr. "Time – the Next Source of Competitive Advantage." *Harvard Business Review* (July–August 1988): 41–51.

—"The Ten Rules of Effective Research." *The Wall Street Journal* (May 30, 1989).